T0345820

SINGAPORE

An atlas of
PERPETUAL TERRITORIAL TRANSFORMATION

Rodolphe De Koninck, Julie Drolet and Marc Girard

NUS PRESS
SINGAPORE

© 2008 NUS Press
    National University of Singapore
    AS3-01-02, 3 Arts Link
    Singapore 117569

    Fax: (65) 6774-0652
    E-mail: nusbooks@nus.edu.sg
    Website: http://www.nus.edu.sg/npu

ISBN 978-9971-69-39-78 (Cloth)

National Library Board Singapore Cataloguing in Publication Data

Koninck, Rodolphe de.
    Singapore : an atlas of perpetual territorial transformation / Rodolphe De Koninck,
Julie Drolet and Marc Girard. – Singapore : NUS Press, c2008.
p. cm.
Includes bibliographical references.
ISBN-13 : 978-9971-69-39-78

    1. Singapore – Social conditions – Maps.   2. Singapore – Economic conditions –
Maps.   3. Singapore – History – Maps.   4. Land use – Singapore – Maps.   I. Drolet,
Julie, 1982–   II. Girard, Marc, 1964–   III. Title.

G2384.3
912.5957 -- dc22   OCN191658782

Designed by: YW Cheong
Printed by: Mainland Press Pte Ltd

Contents

Preface   v

Introduction: The Territorial Hypothesis   1

Chapter 1 Setting the Stage   5

    PLATE 1   Singapore: A Strategic Location   6
    PLATE 2   Singapore in the Midst of Historical Trade Centres   8
    PLATE 3   Contemporary Singapore   10

Chapter 2 Taming Nature   13

    PLATE 4   Stretching the Land   14
    PLATE 5   Collecting and Stocking Water   16
    PLATE 6   Diversifying Water Supply Sources   18
    PLATE 7   Holding on to Some Forest   20
    PLATE 8   The Garden City   22
    PLATE 9   The Sea in the City   24

Chapter 3 Reorganising Population Distribution   26

    PLATE 10   Spreading Out the Population   28
    PLATE 11   The Housing Question   30
    PLATE 12   Sembawang: Building a New Town   32
    PLATE 13   Private Quarters   34
    PLATE 14   Readjusting the Distribution of Ethnic Communities   36

Chapter 4 Reorganising Production and Circulation   39

    PLATE 15   Rationing Agriculture   40
    PLATE 16   Expanding and Consolidating Industry   42
    PLATE 17   Jurong: From Mangrove to Industrial Estate   44
    PLATE 18   Petroleum Islands   46
    PLATE 19   Foreign Lands for Expansion: The Riau Islands   48
    PLATE 20   Foreign Lands for Expansion: Johor   50
    PLATE 21   Foreign Lands for Expansion: The World   52
    PLATE 22   Making Way for Cars   54
    PLATE 23   Transporting Workers   56
    PLATE 24   Doors Wide Open to the World   58
    PLATE 25   Changi: An Airport in the Sea   60
    PLATE 26   SIA: A World Class Airline   62

Chapter 5 Services, Control and Entertainment   *65*

    PLATE 27   Places to Pray   66
    PLATE 28   Places for Burial   68
    PLATE 29   Places to Study   70
    PLATE 30   Places for Recreation   72
    PLATE 31   Rallying Points   74
    PLATE 32   The Tourist Trail: Orchard Road   76

Chapter 6 The Perpetual Production of Territory in Singapore   *79*

    PLATE 33   From Master Plan to Revised Model: 1958 to 2003   80
    PLATE 34   Land Use in 2005   82

Conclusion: The Moveable Stage   84

Appendix 1: Dates and Events   85

Appendix 2: Singapore 1959–2006   86

Bibliography   87
    Map and Table Sources   87
    Other Sources   92

About the Authors   96

Preface

The preparation of this essay, which takes the form of an atlas, is the result of a collaborative endeavour. The three authors engaged in numerous work sessions and discussions on the ideal form that the contents and particularly the maps should take. Over the course of the last two years, as each of us was involved in several other ventures, we still managed to get together frequently, in person or through the internet, in order to work on the atlas, and to debate its contents, the validity of the sources available as well as the intricacies of an analysis relying on time series representations. Singapore changes so rapidly, yet in such a generally well monitored fashion, that we frequently had doubts about the need for, as well as the validity of, an analytical atlas. Nevertheless, thanks to encouragement from friends and colleagues, particularly in Singapore and in Montreal, two thriving yet vastly different cities half way around the world from one other, we completed the task. For this we are grateful to many, particularly in those two places, more specifically at the Université de Montréal and at the National University of Singapore.

We also wish to thank the Groupement d'Intérêt Public (GIP) Reclus, in Montpellier, France, which published in 1992 the bilingual *Singapour: Un atlas de la révolution du territoire / Singapore: An Atlas of the Revolution of Territory*, authored by Rodolphe De Koninck. The GIP gracefully granted us permission to make use of the original map files as did the Éditions Belin for the map files adapted to produce plates 19, 20, 21 and 26. Finally, we express our gratitude to the Social Sciences and Humanities Research Council of Canada for its financial support.

Montreal, January 2008

Introduction: The Territorial Hypothesis

At times the contemplation of the attitudes of the people of Singapore drives one to tears, more often it leaves one in a state of stunned and slightly resentful admiration. — D. J. Enright, 1969, p. 181

An observer of the Singaporean scene can hardly remain indifferent: he might be fascinated or shocked but never disinterested. Weary or still curious Asia scholars, disillusioned or militant development specialists, ignorant or well informed tourists, all are impressed with the dynamism of the small island republic, by what is done away with as well as by what is being achieved in the midst of what appears to be a perpetual transformation. Indeed, for now close to fifty years – and particularly since 1965, when it became a fully independent city-state – Singapore has been an effervescent laboratory of economic, social and environmental transformation and innovation, with its political rulers appearing remarkably stable, even conservative, and its inhabitants apparently consensual.

Studies dealing with these changes are quite numerous. Occasionally carried out by foreigners, they are more frequently authored by local citizens, particularly civil servants or academics. Generally published in the form of readers, such works, while mentioning the magnitude of the environmental transformations, seem to consider them as an inevitable consequence of the Singaporean nation building process. The reasoning goes somewhat as follows: the island of Singapore being small (currently about 720 sq km), the needs and ambitions of its citizens being great, the former must be thoroughly transformed and extended.

Legitimate in itself, this interpretation – which is in full compliance with that of the authorities – leaves no room for the following hypothesis: the remarkable and much vaunted efficiency in the implementation of socio-economic transformations, even more so the tranquility with which the Singaporean population seems to live through them, are at least partly attributable to the permanent transformation of its living space. According to this hypothesis (formulated more fully in De Koninck, 1990 and 1992), the manipulation of the environment and the repeated erosion or ephemeral character of all spatial bearings at the local level allow for only one level of territorial allegiance: that of the Republic of Singapore. The constant redefinition of these spatial and environmental bearings, while associated with other forms of monitoring, and not necessarily the result of a concerted decision, is not a mere consequence of changes accomplished in the political, economic and social spheres, but rather a tool. Spatial instability and territorial alienation at the local level foster social docility or at least assent. Short of relying on a massive survey of *topophilia* (from the Greek words *topos* and *philia*, for place and love, hence literally meaning love of place, or sense of place) among Singaporeans, such a hypothesis would be difficult to verify. But its validity can at least be emphasised by an illustration of the nature and magnitude of the permanent transformations that, since the early 1960s, seem to have become an inevitable feature of the Singaporean landscape.

We may add that the territorial hypothesis does not result from a fortuitous hunch, but rather from a reflection that originated nearly forty years ago when the first author was pursuing his PhD studies at the University of Singapore. For his thesis research (1967–70), which dealt with the Chinese market gardeners then still active in the Singaporean countryside, he roamed across the entire island and became somewhat aware of the transformation that was in the making (De Koninck, 1975). But it was only after several additional and mostly brief sojourns between 1972 and 1989, when Singapore no longer represented for him a privileged object of study, that the magnitude of the changes really began to bewilder him. Losing his way or having difficulty with directions in an environment which had once been so familiar brought the following questions to his mind. How can such a pace be maintained? How do the citizens of this country, who possess such rich cultural backgrounds, accept the fact that the very ground on which they live is perpetually changing, that the carpet is constantly pulled from under their feet? How – notwithstanding the obvious improvements in their standards of living – do they cope with the near constant removal or transformation of their landmarks? All the answers to my questions, all the studies consulted, remained unsatisfactory. Then a new interrogation took form: somewhat like the case of the earth's revolutions around its axis, rapid and definitive to the point where most people do not attempt to understand its movement, aren't the average Singaporeans caught in such a whirlwind that they have no choice but to hang on ... or drop off?

To substantiate this interrogation further, documentary as well as field research was carried out in Singapore in 1990. It led to the production of a first edition of this atlas, essentially dedicated to the illustration of the whirling territorial redistributions. Published in France in 1992 in a bilingual version (French and English), that initial book is now out of print. But Singapore's way of doing things hasn't changed. On the contrary, the perpetual transformation of the environment, in any form – physical, urban, rural, residential, infrastructural, cultural, etc. – is still proceeding apace. In other words, the territorial hypothesis still seems applicable. The permanent overhaul of the Singaporean environment, whether one calls it development, improvement or upgrading, still seems to be a way of life, or rather a way of managing a country – since some may call it governance. But now the country is definitely prosperous and therefore a place where constant and rapid territorial transformation does not appear so indispensable, so obviously urgent. Hence this thoroughly revised and updated edition of the 1992 volume the first author published in 1992 under the title *An Atlas of the Revolution of Territory*.

We still hypothesise that the systematic overhaul of the Singaporean environment represents a deliberate and politically motivated form of social transformation and social management, a transformation monitored from above. To further document the validity of this territorial hypothesis, we redesigned and updated the maps produced in 1992. Following this examination of several forms of apparently systematic and permanent territorial upheavals, we conclude with a spatial model "par excellence", that of a State in perpetually planned and replanned transformation, constantly having to adapt itself to models of its own making.

Four additional basic comments are necessary. First, this atlas is not meant to be comprehensive and even less to act as a reference work. Rather, it constitutes an essay, an attempt to consolidate a hypothesis relying on an original approach and making use of relatively broad and primarily cartographic source material. Second, just like the atlas itself, the individual maps along with their comments are not meant to cover the whole ground, whether about industry, housing or tourism – all topics on which statistics quickly become outdated in Singapore, even less the whole of the Singaporean "project" and its underlying social and political philosophy. The choice of topics and manner of their handling were largely determined by their potential contribution to the illustration of the territorial hypothesis. Third, several potentially interesting themes could not be addressed. In some cases, such as electoral constituency maps, this was because of the political sensitivity of the issue. In other cases, we were faced with lack of data, particularly comparable data allowing for the representation of time series. Fourth, for the themes retained, available data did not always concern identical years, although, for most of them we did try and favour a diachronic and even more a "triachronic" representation.

It remains quite evident that an attempt to comprehend the permanently animated Singaporean scene could rely on much more elaborate illustrations, at a variety of scales, including that of neighbourhoods and even streets, at least those that can still be retraced. Nevertheless, the illustrations that follow do suggest some keys.

1

Setting the Stage

This is by far the most important station in the East; and, as far as naval superiority and commercial interests are concerned, of much higher value than whole continents of territory. — Stamford Raffles, 1819 (in Turnbull, 1989, p. 12)

From age to age, a port had arisen in this part of the Malay world. ... In the past, such cities had been dominated by Malay rulers and the maritime peoples of the region. In the nineteenth century, even though it was under British rule, Singapore shared fully in the trans-Asian, maritime trading culture that had a heritage of over fifteen centuries. — Carl A. Trocki, 2006, p. 9

The British asserted their control over Singapore in 1819, thanks to Stamford Raffles, who, in the name of the *East India Company*, established a trading post which was soon to thrive, halfway between Calcutta, the capital of the British Indian Empire, and Canton, the main gate to China. As early as 1823, even before the conclusion of the 1824 Treaty of London granting Melaka to the British, the island's population had grown from a mere few hundreds to more than 10,000. The opening of the Suez Canal in 1869 consolidated its trading function in the service of British colonial interests. A free port and emporium surrounded by resource rich territories, Singapore was both a haven and a transit place for immigrants. Its destiny was associated with that of the Malay Peninsula, where tin and eventually rubber were produced in vast quantities. The opening of a large naval base in 1923 was followed shortly by the establishment of two Royal Air Force bases. That did not prevent "Fortress Singapore" from collapsing under the Japanese attack of February 1942. In 1945, after more than three years of occupation, demographic growth, which had reached unprecedented levels during the 1930s, resumed. Overcrowding of the urban core, particularly Chinatown, and of the major suburbs became acute, with one third of the entire population living in slums. By the end of the 1950s, as poverty, crime, social conflicts and political unrest increased, the situation had become explosive. For the Singaporean political leaders, solutions had to be found. Among these, the territorial revolution soon became an essential one.

PLATE 1

Singapore: A Strategic Location

It has almost become a truism to refer to Singapore as being strategically located. Yet, truism or not, among major cities on the planet, Singapore is indeed among the most strategically located. And that applies at several scales. To begin with, it stands at the very tip of the Malay Peninsula, which constitutes the ultimate southern projection of the Asian continent. As such, it nearly straddles the Equator and is located at the junction of the Pacific and Indian Oceans. More fundamentally, it occupies, in calm equatorial and well-sheltered waters, a commanding position at the southern extremity of the Strait of Malacca, the key passage between these two oceans. It therefore stands in a nodal position on the sea route linking East and South Asia, the so-called China Road. To this function as a commanding stopover on the world's busiest sea route – and also its busiest port – has recently been added its role as an airline hub between Eurasia and Australasia. Finally, within Southeast Asia itself, Singapore occupies a key position at the core of the archipelago, or more precisely at the heart of the Malay world between Malaysia and Indonesia.

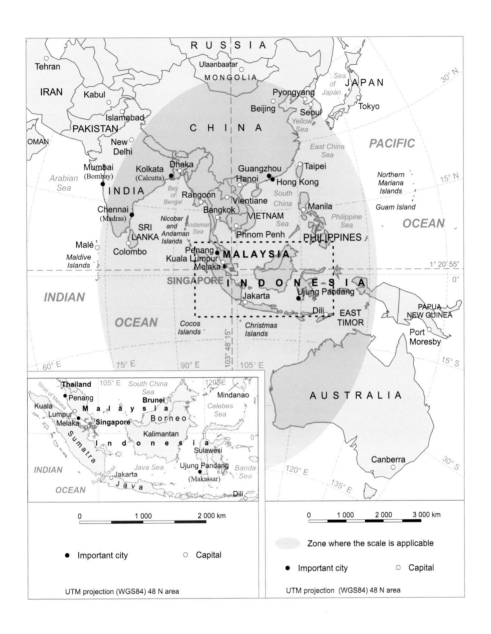

PLATE 2

Singapore in the Midst of Historical Trade Centres

Situated some 140 km north of the Equator, the island of Singapore occupies a sheltered position at the southern end of the Malay Peninsula and of the Strait of Malacca Throughout history, for reasons related as much to navigation and settlement as to the policies of empires, this passage became the most important link between the Indian and Pacific Oceans and a key one on the world's surface. Nevertheless, even if ships had long sailed through the Strait of Malacca, Singapore began to play a particularly eminent role only after the founding of the British trading post in 1819 by Stamford Raffles. It then quickly became an essential component of the British Empire and of its trading network with the Far East. Earlier, its own history had been overshadowed by that of various states and kingdoms having exercised some form of hegemony in the region: in particular Srivijaya, Siam and the sultanates of Aceh, Melaka and Johor. Recent archaeological and historical findings confirm that from the end of the thirteenth century until the early fifteenth, the island had probably been the seat of a Malay kingdom, which, in 1320, hosted an envoy from the Yuan Emperor. Under the name of Temasek, or of Singapura (Lion City) in use from the end of that century, it was subsequently known as a refuge for pirates, like many surrounding archipelagos, islands and estuaries. A closer look at the maze of islands that spread between Sumatra and the Malay Peninsula reveals the quality of Singapore Island's sheltered location, arguably much preferable to those of other historical trade centres found in the region, whether in the nearby Riau Archipelago or on the coast and estuaries of the Peninsula or of Sumatra Island.

PLATE 3

Contemporary Singapore

To facilitate the consultation of the series of plates that follow, we have grouped here three reference maps. The first one, dealing with topography, is in fact a virtual one or rather an historical and composite one. The topography represented on it was largely extracted from 1966 topographical maps and from a map produced by Wong Poh Poh in 1966 at the Geography Department of what was then the University of Singapore. Given the lack of comprehensive topographical maps currently available, we have adapted that "historical" information to fit the contemporary contours of the main island. The map shows that, while Singapore was never mountainous, it was and still remains far from flat, with several ranges of hills structuring the territory, particularly at its geographical core. This renders even more astonishing the extensive transformations administered, so to speak, to the island over the last four decades.

The administrative district map provides a reference for place names. The districts correspond to the so-called DGP zones defined in the Urban Redevelopment Authority Development Guide Plans. They are grouped under five regions, to which must be added the central area and two Water Catchment districts. They were used in the 2000 census, the latest one to date. This map provides a number of place names, many of which will not be repeated in the rest of the book, and is therefore useful for the consultation of many of the maps that it contains.

The third map illustrates the extent to which Singapore is highly urbanised, to a point where it indeed deserves the appellation city-state. It represents a gross simplification of the information provided in the very detailed 2005 Land Use map (see Plate 34). Thus the "built-up" land use category encompasses nearly everything, except open and green spaces, agricultural areas, areas to be developed such as those recently reclaimed from the sea and, finally, military areas: these are rather extensive in districts such as the Western Water Catchment (the largest), Mandai, Seletar and Paya Lebar.

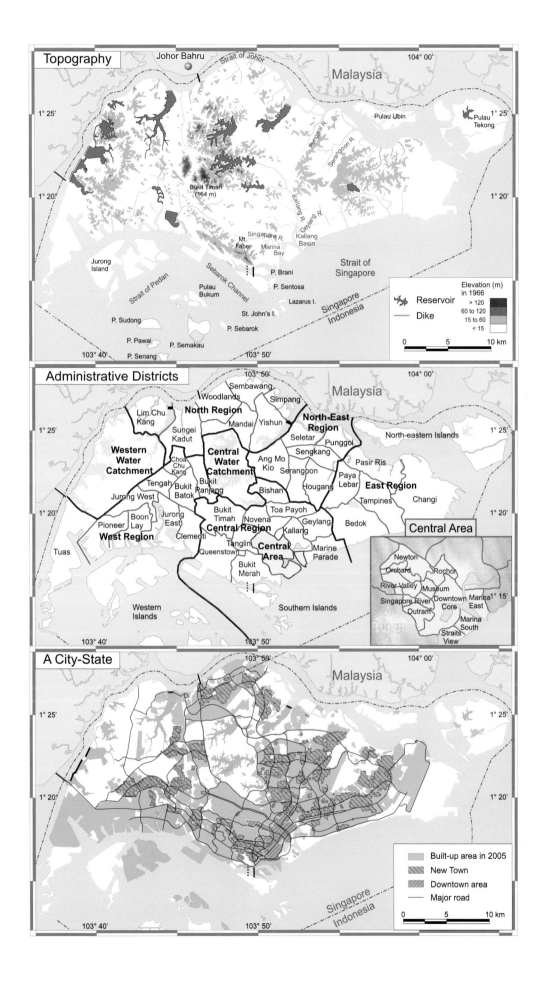

2

Taming nature

I sent research teams to visit botanical gardens, public parks and arboreta in the tropical and subtropical zones .... Our botanists brought back 8,000 different varieties and got some 2,000 to grow in Singapore. ... Greening is the most cost-effective project I ever launched. — Lee Kuan Yew, 2000, pp. 177–8

Planned environmental transformations are not new to Singapore. Shortly after settling on the island in 1819, the British remodelled the banks of the Singapore river estuary, filling in the surrounding swamps. Throughout the nineteenth century, along with the harbour's development, came further drainage, land filling, even land reclamation along the coast extending south-west of that estuary. The earth used for the seaward expansion of the island was collected from the hills in the hinterland. Mostly confined to the harbour and city area, such earthworks continued during the first half of the twentieth century. Some transformations also took place on the north shore of the island, near the one kilometre long causeway leading to the Malay Peninsula that was constructed in 1923, as well as further east to accommodate the Sembawang air and naval base, also built in 1923.

But it is the postcolonial administration, beginning in 1959, and even more after the founding of the Republic of Singapore in 1965, that initiated the real overhaul, what was to become a permanent process. It first concerned the very shape and dimension not only of the island of Singapore itself, but also of the other 60-odd smaller islands that were part of the national territory. Not only size and shape were taken to task but also regional and local functions. Some areas previously covered with swamps, such as most of the south-western portion of the island, were filled in to accommodate an industrial estate. On the eastern flank, land was gained on the sea so as to allow for the relocation of what was soon to become one of Asia's key airports. Out at sea, islands were evacuated and some were extended or regrouped to host the petroleum industry. Even the central urban area was largely transformed to take in seawater bodies and integrate them in the city's landscape. More fundamentally, large portions of the island, in all directions, became susceptible to being transformed, and many were to host New Towns as part of a very audacious housing policy that spearheaded the national overhaul.

PLATE 4

Stretching the Land

Over the last 30 years or so, Singapore's land mass has gained some 140 sq km at the expense of the sea. This represents an increase in size of nearly 25 per cent. Originally, and until the late 1960s, the main sources of landfill were local hills. These were levelled to provide the earth needed to "stretch" the island. More recently landfill has been obtained, purchased to be exact, from the Indonesian islands that make up the nearby Riau and Lingga archipelagos, and by dredging the sea bottom within Singapore's territorial waters. This process has brought about a radical transformation of the relief and even more of the outline of the main island and its satellites, particularly the Western Islands. On these are concentrated most of the country's petroleum tanks, refineries and other petrochemical infrastructure. The striking transformation of Singapore Island's coastline is not solely caused by its territorial extension through land filling or reclamation, but also by the closure of the estuaries of the main rivers draining the interior of the island. Also applied to the swamps encircling part of the island, particularly on the western flank, this dike construction has also made possible the creation of additional fresh water reservoirs, such as those at Kranji and Seletar, once the newly created basins were desalinated.

Singapore's need for landfill has created disputes with its nearest neighbours. In 2003, because of environmental concerns and, supposedly, border delineation issues, Indonesia banned the export of marine sand to Singapore, and in January 2007 widened the ban to include all types of sand and soil. Malaysia had protested against the expansion of the island of Tekong and the Tuas peninsula at either end of the Strait of Johor. Nevertheless, the expansion is expected to continue, with, according to Singapore's 2003 Master Plan, an additional 50-odd sq km to be gained at the expense of the country's territorial waters.

Year	1957	1980	1990	1999	2006	2008[a]
Land area in sq km	581	617.8	633	659.9	722.6	775.5

a. Master Plan

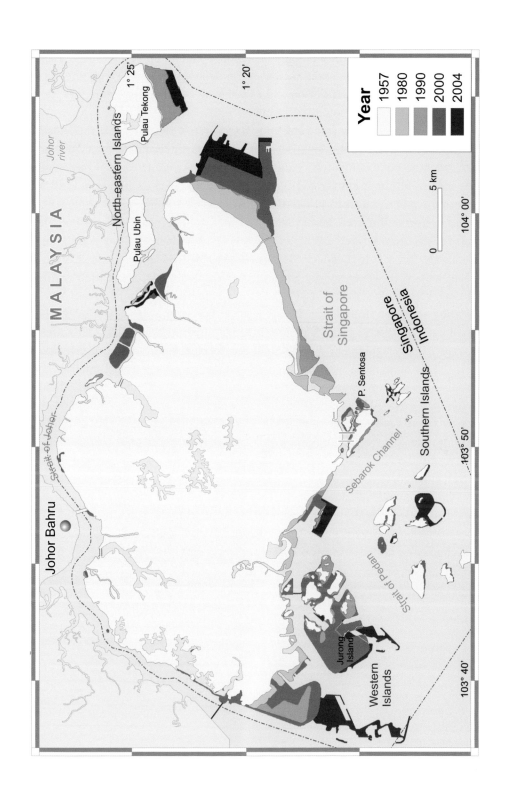

PLATE 5

Collecting and Stocking Water

With its typically equatorial climate, Singapore's annual precipitation is abundant, the different regions of the island receiving on average from 230 to 260 centimetres of rain, the drainage, redistribution and evacuation of which is insured by a constantly improved network of impressive canals.

Even with so much rainwater, the small island republic still falls short of self-sufficiency in fresh water supplies. Although the government over the last decades has led numerous campaigns calling on Singaporeans to save water, consumption has increased much more rapidly than population. In fact, between 1960 and 2006, a period when the overall population (residents and non-residents) less than tripled, water consumption grew more than fivefold. The discrepancy is attributable to rapid industrialisation as well as to an overall improvement in the population's living standards. As a consequence, Singapore has had to acquire, at least until recently, about half of its water supply from the Malay Peninsula, a situation dating back to the colonial days. As early as 1931, a water pipeline was built across the causeway to bring in water from Johor. In 1961, even before the formation of the Federation of Malaysia (1963) – which included Singapore for two years – Singapore signed a water supply agreement with the state of Johor that was valid in principle for 100 years. This agreement was modified the following year but still guaranteed a cheap supply of water for Singapore. In the late 1980s, the government of the island republic actually purchased an entire 150 sq km watershed, some 20 km inland, a third of which was transformed into a reservoir. The Singaporeans then built a water treatment plant on the spot, relayed by pipeline 90 per cent of the treated water to the city-state and resold the rest to the Johor government, apparently generating enough revenue to cover Singapore's costs.

On the island side, massive works were launched to improve water storage facilities. In 1960, the main island had only three large fresh water reservoirs, all located in its centre and covering less than 4 sq km. Today, there exist fifteen reservoirs – to which must be added several so-called service reservoirs – more dispersed and considerably larger, with a combined surface area of some 28 sq km.

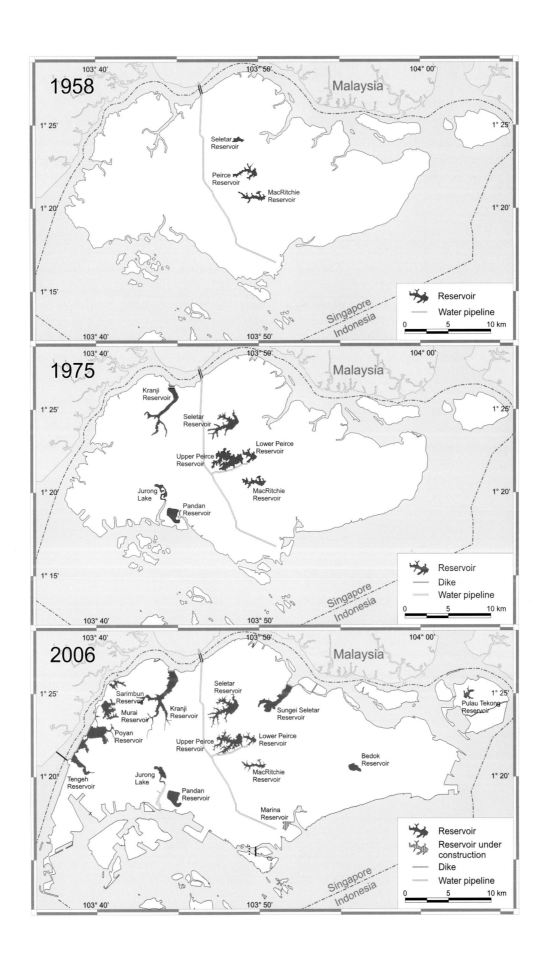

PLATE 6

Diversifying Water Supply Sources

Notwithstanding this impressive expansion of local water storage capacity, the Singaporean water deficit problem remains very serious, and takes on added significance whenever the Malaysian authorities attempt to renegotiate the previous agreements. In this context, the government continues to search for solutions. In the early 1990s, a water tanker service operated between the Indonesian island of Bintan and the Singaporean "mainland", but that did not last long. The city-state needed to find better and more reliable ways of achieving self-sufficiency. This quest has taken several forms, including better monitoring of water catchments and storage areas, as well as construction of desalination plants and so-called NeWater plants. While the former – so far only one has been established, in 2005, in the Tuas peninsula – processes sea water, the latter actually treat and recycle used water, hence the name NeWater. Four NeWater plants are currently in operation, the first two having been opened in 2003 and the latest in 2007. The results have been quite impressive: in 2000 local sources supplied some 53 per cent of national needs; for 2007, the figure will be close to 75 per cent.

Years	Water Consumption Per Annum (in m³)
1960	99,482,000
1970	152,943,000
1980	216,566,000
1990	322,798,000
2000	55,488,000
2006	509,000,000

National Sources of Water Supply	2000	2007
Local Water Catchments (m³/day)	680,000	680,000
NeWater (m³/day)	–	236,000
Desalinated Water (m³/day)	–	136,000
Total (m³/day)	680,000	1,052,000
TOTAL (m³/year)	248,200,000	383,980,000

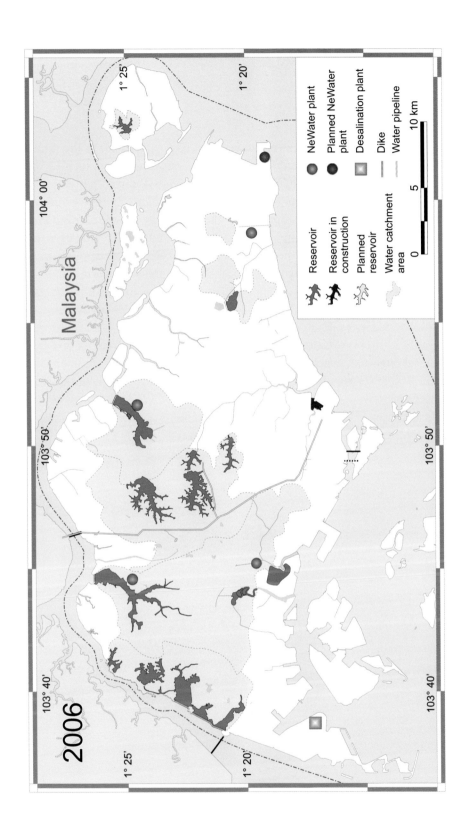

2006

Malaysia

● NeWater plant	● Reservoir
● Planned NeWater plant	● Reservoir in construction
▣ Desalination plant	● Planned reservoir
— Dike	⬚ Water catchment area
— Water pipeline	

0   5   10 km

104° 00'   103° 50'   103° 40'

1° 25'   1° 20'

1° 25'   1° 20'

PLATE 7

Holding on to Some Forest

Although a vigorous tree planting campaign, covering not only the recreation areas but also residential, commercial and industrial ones, has accompanied urban expansion, natural forests have inexorably retreated. This occurred particularly during the 1970s, when mangrove forests were considerably reduced. In fact, stands of mangrove were essentially wiped out from the southern islands and all along the western and south-western coasts and estuaries, mostly to open land for industrial installations. In the south-western part of the island, all inland forests also disappeared. The forest cover in the hilly centre of the island shrank during the same period, much of it giving way to reservoirs. But it is still substantial and retains today small strips of primary forest – in particular the 164 hectares of the Bukit Timah Nature Reserve (established in 1883) – while residual patches of mangrove are found in several locations along the northern shores. More substantial stands remain on the shores of Pulau Ubin and Pulau Tekong, and, especially, on the north-western coast of the main island, in the Sungei Buloh Wetland Reserve (created in 1989), which has been transformed into a nature park.

In addition to these older forests, a large number of new parks had been developed, contributing to the greening of Singapore.

Year	1960	1985	2006
Area covered by natural forests in km²	37.8	28.6	22.64

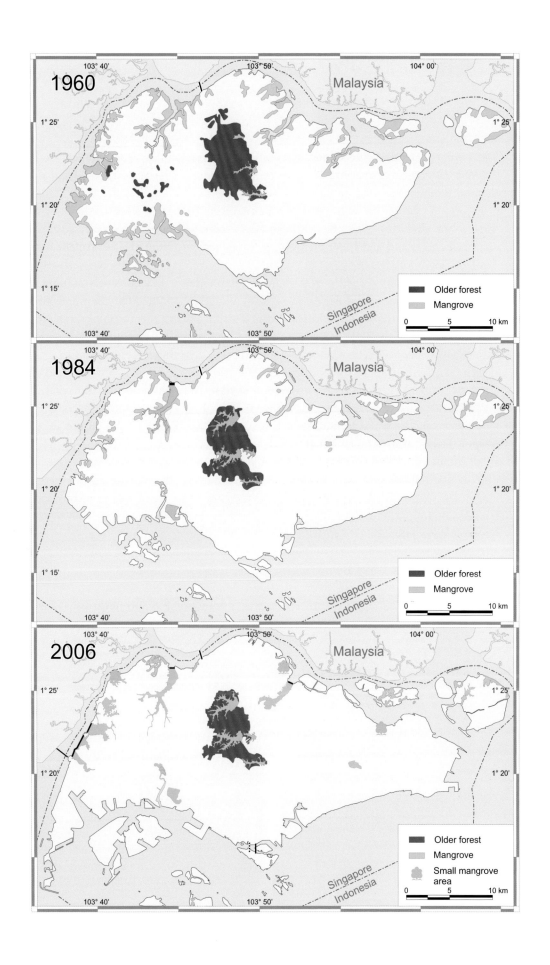

PLATE 8

The Garden City

The retreat of natural forests and of agricultural land use has been balanced to some extent by a constant greening of the City and, in fact, of large portions of the island. Several of the remaining patches of natural forest have been either designated as or transformed into parks, with recreational facilities being installed in some of them. Such is the case, for example, with the Bukit Timah Nature Reserve, located in the centre of the island and itself centred on the island's summit (Bukit Timah, literally Tin Hill, 164 m high).

In addition, a number of new parks was established – they currently number more than 60 and cover a total of nearly 20 sq km – including some in the central urban area where remarkable parks had already been laid out during the colonial days. One of these is Fort Canning Park, at the top of Fort Canning Hill, a key historical landmark, called Government Hill in the early colonial days (see Plate 9), and Bukit Larangan (Forbidden Hill) prior to that. Another is the truly extraordinary 47-hectare Botanic Gardens, whose original version was established in 1822 on the slopes of Government Hill. The expansion of green parks also occurred along the coasts, especially the south-east one, with the longitudinal East Coast Park. Since 1971 – at the initiative of then Prime Minister Lee Kuan Yew – each November the population participates in an Annual Tree Planting Day. In this manner, hundreds of thousands of trees were planted, including along roads and highways, to an extent probably unknown anywhere else in the world. Finally, a network of pathways linking green spaces throughout the island is being put into place. These park connectors will eventually stretch to several hundred kilometres.

The government obviously takes Singapore's green heritage very seriously. Since 1996, the National Parks Board has coordinated its maintenance and expansion. The latter exercises jurisdiction over all green spaces, whether forest reserves, parks and recreation areas or park connectors, which total some 8,300 hectares of land (or 83 sq km), nearly 12 per cent of the national territory.

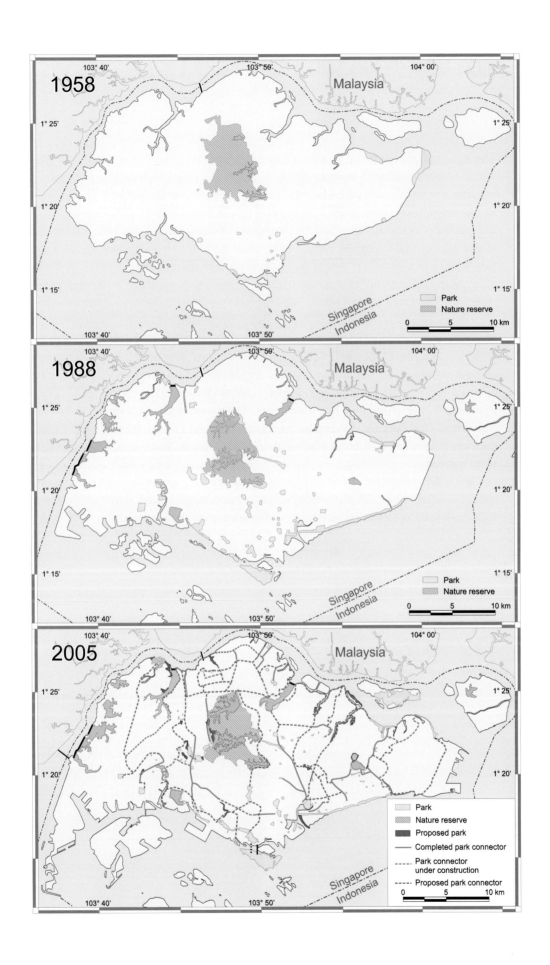

PLATE 9

The Sea in the City

The seaward expansion of the Singaporean shoreline concerns not only the island's south-western and south-eastern reaches, which until the 1950s were still largely rural, but also the urban core, the Central Business District or Downtown Core. The latter has developed on either side of the mouth of the Singapore River, where the original colonial city and its Asian "suburbs" were laid out on a narrow coastal plain at the foot of low lying hills. Today the river, which until the early 1970s flowed directly into the sea, discharges its waters into a bay surrounded by two large expanses of reclaimed land, Marina East and Marina South. Its waters have been cleaned, and its course rectified. The same is true of the Kallang and Geylang Rivers, and the swampy and contaminated basin from which the Kallang River formerly emerged has been filled in. These waterways now converge on Marina Bay – currently being transformed into a fresh water reservoir – and Kallang Basin, and are surrounded by walkways, parks and playgrounds, all planted with trees, bushes and flowers. The grid of the former colonial city, neatly represented on the celebrated Coleman map of 1837, has been maintained, but it has lost its waterfront. Paradoxically, in its quest to become an Equatorial Garden City, Singapore, the great harbour city, is increasingly turning its back on the sea, at least in its historical core, and Beach Road is now three kilometres from the sea.

With the integration of sea space into Singapore's territory, coastal swamps and estuaries along the island's periphery have been transformed into freshwater reservoirs through dike construction and desalination (see Plates 5 and 6).

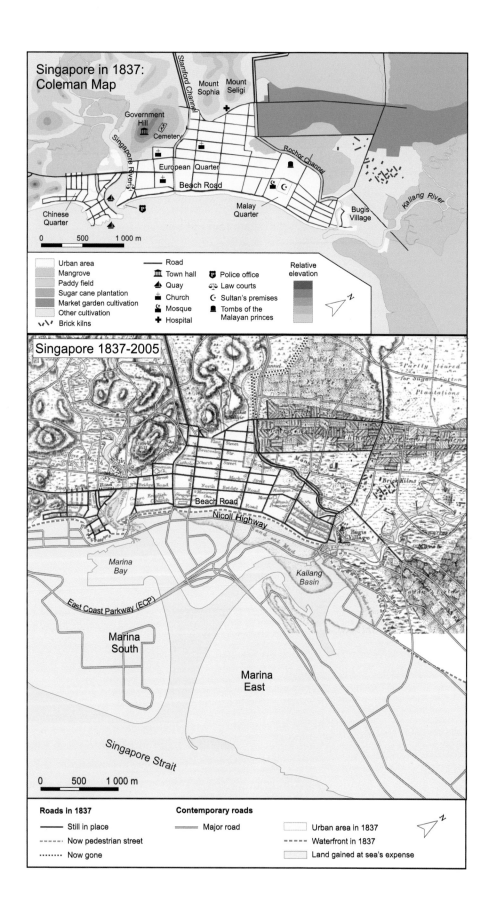

Singapore in 1837: Coleman Map

Mount Sophia
Mount Seligi

Government Hill
Cemetery

European Quarter

Beach Road

Chinese Quarter

Malay Quarter

Bugis Village

Stamford Channel

Singapore River

Rochor Channel

Kallang River

0 500 1 000 m

Urban area	Road		Police office	Relative elevation
Mangrove	🏛 Town hall	🏵	Law courts	
Paddy field	⚓ Quay		Sultan's premises	
Sugar cane plantation	⛪ Church		Tombs of the Malayan princes	
Market garden cultivation	🕌 Mosque			
Other cultivation	✚ Hospital			
Brick kilns				

Singapore 1837-2005

Beach Road

Nicoll Highway

Marina Bay

Kallang Basin

East Coast Parkway (ECP)

Marina South

Marina East

Singapore Strait

0 500 1 000 m

Roads in 1837

—— Still in place

----- Now pedestrian street

········ Now gone

Contemporary roads

══ Major road

Urban area in 1837

----- Waterfront in 1837

Land gained at sea's expense

3

Reorganising Population Distribution

The Singapore of today is the direct result of the modernizing zeal of the first generation of post colonial leaders. They are men not given to cosmic dreams or grand ideologies. They are practical realists. Thus the achievements of the state, the vindication of its policies and the symbols of success that now exist are in the form of the material development of the state, as for instance in the ever-present high-rise public-housing estates. Indeed public housing in Singapore is the single most visible index of the government's outstanding performance; it is the de facto *monument to the People's Action Party government's success. There is no need for another. —* Tay Kheng Soon, 1989a, p. 860

Since the early 1960s and particularly after independence in 1965, the Singapore authorities have maintained the national territory under a state of permanent upheaval. This has been rendered possible thanks to special assets, including a sizeable land bank inherited from the colonial administration in 1959 (crown land), equivalent to a third of the country's surface area. To this was added an additional 10 per cent of the country's territory, made available as the British military bases were gradually closed down (1968–1971), a few years after Singapore separated from Malaysia (1965). Even more important for development or redevelopment, a series of laws – the Land Acquisition Ordnance (1955), Land Acquisition Act (1966), Property Tax Order (1967), and Control Premises Bill (1968) – gave the state legal powers to exercise eminent domain over practically the entire national territory. Armed with this authority, various government agencies and in particular the Housing and Development Board were able to expropriate as they saw fit, and they exercised this power freely.

The result has simply been astonishing. All types of property in all parts of the island, rural as well as urban, were and remain subject to expropriation. The relative intensity of operations varies from one region to another, according to the different demolition and development programmes, with the urbanised centre of the main island frequently targeted. An expropriation site might be a vacant lot, an agricultural plot or a building, or an entire village or residential block whose occupants – in the earlier days they were often squatters – are invited to relocate while receiving financial compensation. Several sites have been the object of more than one operation of expropriation-evacuation-demolition-reconstruction. During a period of just over twenty years, from 1965 to 1988, well over 1,200 sites were selected for expropriation and nearly 270,000 families were displaced, about a third of the country's population.

While the methods have evolved, and the costs and compensations greatly increased, the general principle still prevails. All over the national territory, dwellings may be acquired for upgrading or demolition and replacement, and when this occurs the occupants are required to sell and relocate. As people move, so do their schools, markets, places of worship and recreational areas. In this manner, some regions are emptied of their population while others rapidly become heavily populated.

PLATE 10

Spreading out the Population

The relocation of displaced families has brought about a constant geographical redistribution of the national population whose growth has been held in check, although policies on that front have changed on many occasions. Comparing population distribution maps for 1957, 1980 and 2000 provides a striking picture.[1]

In 1957, before the great overhaul began, three quarters of the Colony's population, which then stood at about 1.4 million persons, lived within 8 km of the mouth of the Singapore River, concentrated in the urban core – notably in Chinatown – or in the close suburbs.

By 1980, the 2.4 million inhabitants were already more evenly distributed around the country. The urban core and its immediate periphery had lost half of their residents, and the population there has since continued to decline. Conversely, around this zone a ring of population nuclei had taken form. These were New Towns, created by the Housing and Development Board, whose occupancy has since steadily increased.

In 2000, when the resident population reached nearly 3.3 million persons, the overall occupation of the national territory appeared even more balanced. The decongestion of the old urban core had continued while several new outlying population nuclei had been created, notably in the North and North-East regions. Concurrently, several areas, including whole districts, had been largely emptied of their inhabitants.[2] Such was the case of the entire western flank of the island, particularly the Tuas, Western Water Catchment and Lim Chu Kang districts and, on the eastern side, the areas surrounding Changi airport.

---

1. The census figures used here take only permanent residents into account. In 2000, in addition to the permanent residents who numbered some 3,263,000, there were an estimated 650,000 non-permanent residents in Singapore. Today, that estimated figure surpasses 800,000.
2. The method used does not allow for the representation of small numbers, with one dot accounting for at least 500 persons. This means that the apparently empty regions can possibly be inhabited by small numbers of residents.

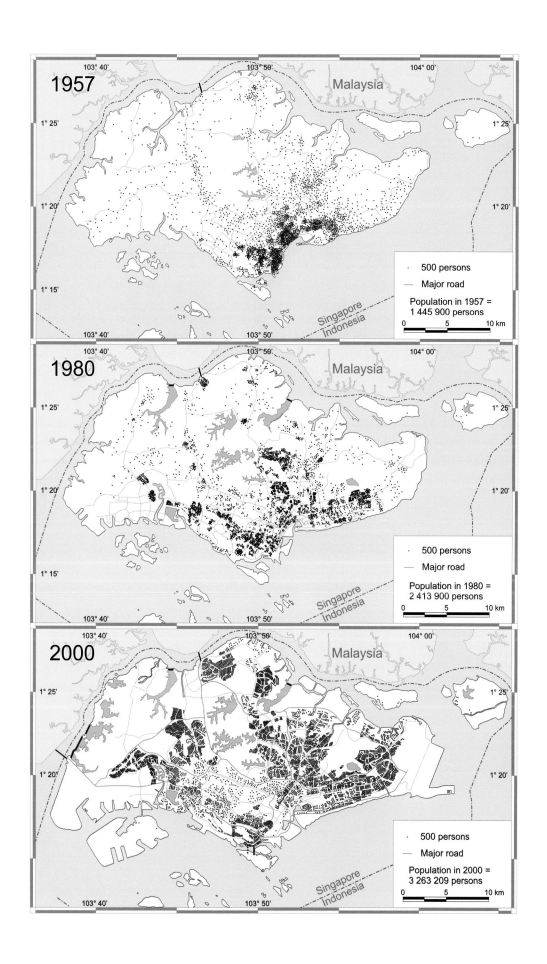

PLATE 11

The Housing Question

In 1960, when the Housing and Development Board (HDB) was established, the resolution of the "housing question" was placed on an equal footing with the restructuring of the economy as indispensable to national survival. Often praised, sometimes criticised, the creation of New Towns has since been the spearhead for the Singaporean territorial overhaul. A State within the State, the HDB has at its disposal an enormous budget along with wide powers to dispossess people and develop housing estates. Not only does it manage the largest national land bank, it is also by far the country's richest and most powerful landlord. In 1959, less than 9 per cent of the population were sheltered in public housing, still the responsibility of the Singapore Improvement Trust formed in 1927 under colonial administration. By 1974, nearly 43 per cent of the population lived in HDB flats, and by 1989 the proportion had reached 87 per cent, that is, 2.3 million persons. That proportion then began to fall back as the share of private estates increased, along with the average Singaporean's purchasing power. By 2005, the share of public housing stood at about 80 per cent.

A total of 26 New Towns are dispersed throughout the island, and they cover more than 18,000 hectares, or a quarter of the national territory. Less than 30 per cent of that land is actually devoted to residential use. Population densities vary considerably from one New Town to another, depending on things such as the height of housing towers and the size of recreation areas. Since the steady transfer of population towards the public housing estates began, the HDB has introduced many changes within its empire. Types of infrastructure and services offered are frequently modified and improved and so are contractual agreements between the residents and the Board. Since 1964, New Town dwellers have been allowed to purchase their flats, and by 1988 nearly half of the apartments constructed by the HDB were privately owned. Today, among the 880,000 public apartments, the proportion of those owned privately has reached 94 per cent. (Countrywide, home ownership ratio is of the same order, the highest in the world). But this ownership remains conditioned by the Board's prerogatives: the latter still exercises full managerial autonomy as well as a right of veto on any housing transaction. On its premises, probably more than anywhere else in the island republic, Singaporeans are closely supervised.

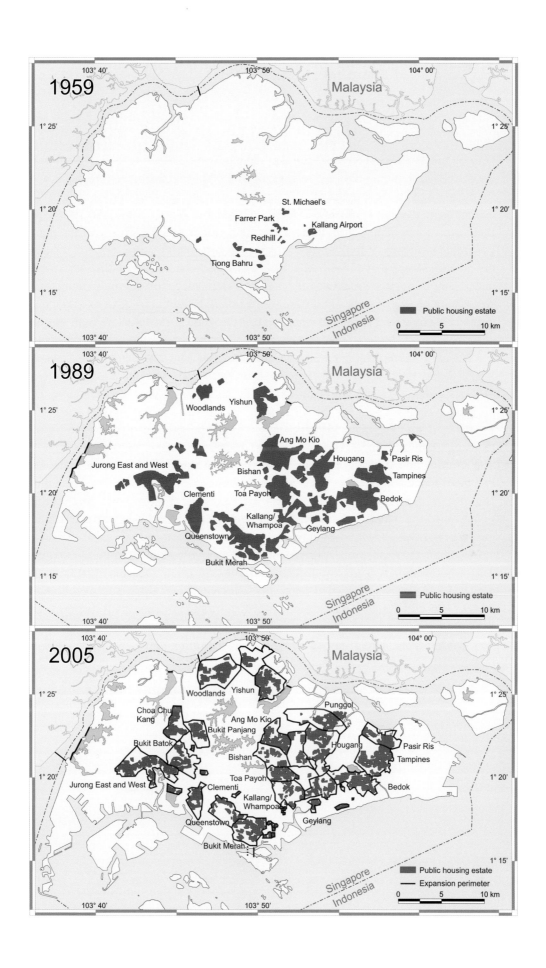

PLATE 12

Sembawang: Building a New Town

One of the goals pursued through the development of public housing estates was decentralisation of population, commercial and industrial infrastructure and activities. As the main instrument in the great Singaporean overhaul, the building of New Towns has inevitably been the object of elaborate planning. For example, the 1971 Concept Plan adopted by the Urban Redevelopment Authority (URA) – another powerful government agency – divided the main island into five planning regions (apart from the Central Area) and identified a centre for each one. One of the key principles underlying this new regionalisation was the creation of relatively autonomous activity areas, with places of work and residential housing brought closer to one another. The decentralisation goal remained important in the 1991 Concept Plan, with the further definition of sub-regional centres served by Mass Rapid Transit (MRT) stations.

It is with these principles in mind that the New Town of Sembawang was established in the 1990s on the northern flank of the island, near the shores of the Johor Strait. Its development was carried out in accordance with the Planning Report of Sembawang adopted by the URA in 1996. In the eponymous northern district, vacant land was available for development, and the site was surrounded by important employment centres. These included industrial estates as well as the Port of Singapore Authority terminal, itself developed on the site of the former naval base and the famous King George VI Dock, dating back to 1938. As is the case with most New Towns, Sembawang was laid out in the time span of a few years, and thoroughly transformed the natural environment; the Sembawang River was straightened and its headwaters filled in, while the surrounding land was flattened.

By 2006, the residential towers of this town were inhabited by some 63,000 persons. This is below the average New Town population, normally well above 100,000 inhabitants and in the most crowded locations – Jurong West, Tampines, Woodlands and Bedok – around 200,000. The residents of Sembawang have at their disposal, among other things, several schools and places of worship, a commercial area, a park and a golf driving range, and a sports complex cum swimming pool. The Woodlands industrial installations lie just beyond its western limits.

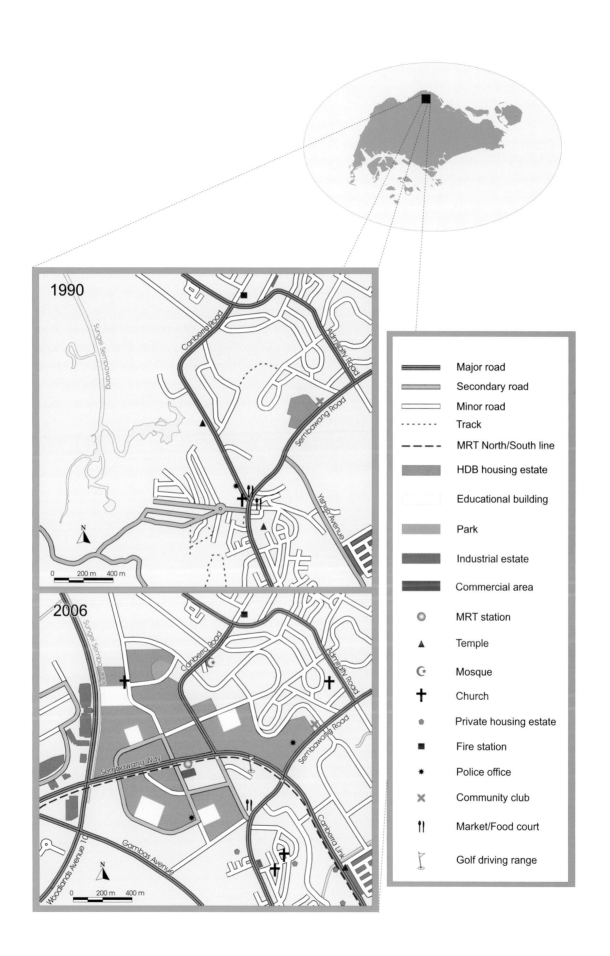

Major road
Secondary road
Minor road
Track
MRT North/South line
HDB housing estate
Educational building
Park
Industrial estate
Commercial area

◎ MRT station
▲ Temple
☪ Mosque
✝ Church
⬠ Private housing estate
■ Fire station
✳ Police office
✕ Community club
🍴 Market/Food court
⛳ Golf driving range

PLATE 13

Private Quarters

The construction industry plays a crucial role in the Singapore economy. Not only is it heavily involved in transport infrastructure construction but also in the development of the hotel industry and as a subcontractor to the HDB, with private housing estates representing an additional lucrative market. Consequently, the sector has enjoyed a nearly uninterrupted boom since at least the mid-1960s; these private "quarters" now house nearly 20 per cent of the country's permanent population. This is largely attributable to the growing affluence of the Singapore population. While in 1959 the number of private housing estates stood at 41, by 1988 it had reached 846, and by 2005 2,071. Over the years, as the massive public housing estates (or New Towns) development programme was receiving all the limelight and a large chunk of public funds – as much as 30 per cent of development funds in the mid-1980s, a lot more than education and defence – the layout of small private housing estates has continued unabated. These are made up of either more spacious and more luxurious residential towers, or only a handful of generally quite comfortable villas or bungalows. Disseminated throughout the urban network, often within close range of the New Towns, they are much less numerous in the outlying areas of the island. Middle class Singaporeans tend to congregate within closer range of the historical urban core.

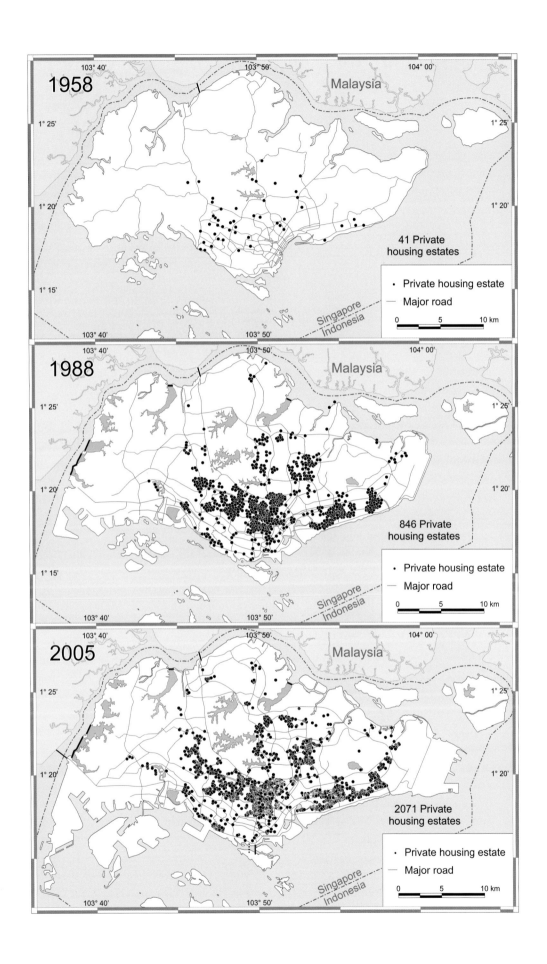

PLATE 14

Readjusting the Distribution of Ethnic Communities

The geographical distribution of ethnic communities represents an issue that has been quite sensitive throughout Singaporean history. The early colonial administration intentionally created ethnic concentrations (see Plate 9), and others emerged as the entire island was gradually occupied. In this way, ethnic areas that were almost ghettos developed not only in the urban core – for example with such well known neighbourhoods as Chinatown, Little India and (Malay) Geylang – but also in the distant countryside, with the East Coast and the outer islands predominantly Malay, and Lim Chu Kang almost exclusively Chinese.

The creation of a sense of national identity transcending ethnic inclinations has long been one of the most commonly reiterated goals of the government. Hence, at least in part, the choice of English as the unifying language in the school system. Hence, also, a policy of population resettlement designed to break up ethnic ghettos, with quotas set to ensure minimal representation of each of the three main ethnic groups in each of the housing estates, taking into account national proportions. According to the 2000 census, these stood at nearly 77 per cent for the Chinese, 14 per cent for the Malays and 8 per cent for the Indians. The precise distribution is hard to verify because the authorities do not reveal figures concerning detailed ethnic geographical distribution at the level of the administrative district, but it seems certain that no group has been exempted or favoured by the massive population redistribution of the last four or five decades, during which the great modern Singaporean overhaul has been implemented.

Moreover, reading and interpreting the maps is complicated by the fact that the administrative grids changed between 1980 and 2000, and by then many districts, more than a dozen, were officially uninhabited, a circumstance that in itself illustrates the magnitude of the population displacement that has taken place. Finally, given the wide discrepancy in the absolute numbers of Chinese, Malays and Indians, with the Chinese much more numerous than the Malays and the Indians, comparisons between the groups are difficult. Nevertheless, while persistence seems to have been the norm, some changes are noticeable. These are the more striking ones revealed by the maps: (1) The largest areas emptied of their resident populations were predominantly Chinese. (2) In the newly industrialised northern districts of Woodlands and Sembawang, Chinese predominance has increased over both the other groups. (3) Major changes in the distribution and number of "places for the Malays" – whether schools, cemeteries or mosques, are particularly perceptible because their original locations were often peripheral. For example, a rapid and drastic transformation occurred in the islands lying to the south of Singapore island, which were evacuated by their inhabitants, most of them Malays. (4) In the central districts of Bukit Timah, Tanglin and Novena, Malay presence has decreased in relative terms. (5) The relative importance of Malays has however been maintained in the easternmost district of Tampines and Changi. (6) The latter district is also the only one were Indians have seen their relative representation increase slightly, possibly because of their greater presence in the service activities related to the Changi Airtropolis.

Chinese

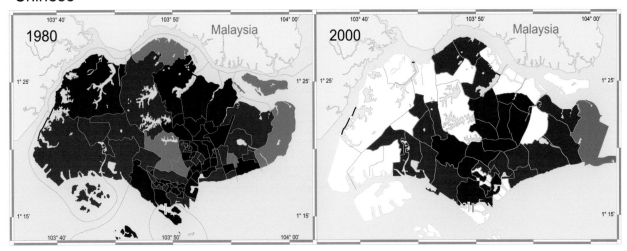

Malays

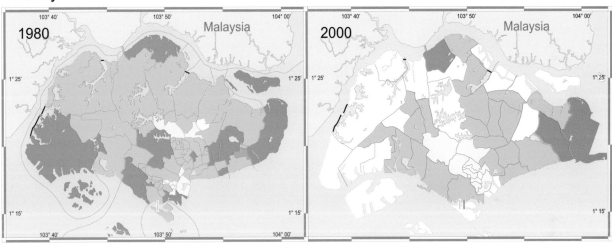

Indians

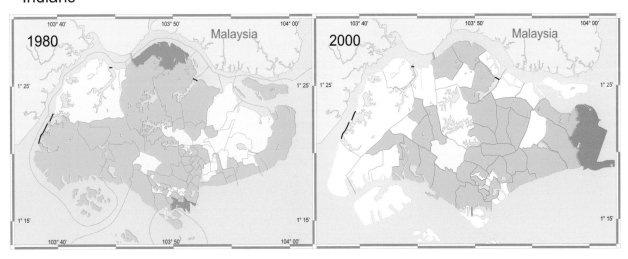

Ethnic communities as a percentage of the population by census district

< 5 %	20-40 %	60-80 %
5-20 %	40-60 %	80-100 %

Uninhabited or non-census area

4

Reorganising Production and Circulation

We have neither a domestic market nor a hinterland. ... To be competitive we must compensate for these disadvantages by offering more. ... Our future lies in being plugged into the international network of trade and communications. — Ministry of Trade and Industry, 1986, p. 12

Since the early 1960s, the directions, shapes, length and nature of the coastlines, the topography, the rivers, water reservoirs, in fact the entire hydrographical networks along with the vegetation cover of the island have been considerably modified. These transformations result from and at the same time render possible a redefinition of the basic functions of production, be they agricultural, commercial or industrial, social reproduction and circulation, all of them closely tied to a new distribution of population, the latter tightly regulated. Concretely, these measures consist of the implementation of numerous urban renewal projects and the development of industrial and housing estates that in turn generate or call for, among other things, new transport networks and recreation infrastructure. This is achieved in a context where the local society and the national economy are fast increasing their links with the outside world. Illustrations are provided by the expansion of the harbour and airport installations as well as by the remarkable growth of the financial sector and even more of telecommunications (not illustrated here). As a result, nearly every locality is thoroughly transformed as it is earmarked for a new function, whether residential, industrial, commercial, recreational or even environmental.

PLATE 15

Rationing Agriculture

In 1960, some 140 sq km, nearly a quarter of the country's territory, were still devoted to agriculture and supplied nearly all of the country's requirements for poultry and pork and half of its vegetables. By 1984, less than 50 sq km of agricultural land remained; two decades later agriculture occupied some 12 sq km, or less than 2 per cent of the territory. Agriculture's extremely rapid rollback was marked by two fundamental characteristics. The first was its total eviction from the immediate periphery of the urban core, the latter having for a long period remained essentially confined to the southern centre of the island. As was to be expected, expansion of the built-up area in other directions was initially achieved at the expense of agricultural land. The second was the partial regrouping, initiated during the 1960s, of agricultural activities in two specific regions of the island: the Lim Chu Kang District and, for a time, the Mandai hills of the North region. The contraction of agricultural land and the resettlement of farm operators were of course carried out in conjunction with urban renewal and industrial estate development. Following the reduction in agricultural land use and employment, overall production declined considerably and irreversibly. Although needing little local space, pig rearing was completely phased out, primarily for ecological reasons, most notably water pollution.

Two types of production, however, flower cultivation, particularly orchids, and some forms of fish rearing, particularly the offshore type, did expand. But fundamentally, just like manufacturing more recently, agriculture and fishing were in many ways relocated abroad, with a growing number of Singapore entrepreneurs contracting out or investing in food production carried out in Malaysia and Indonesia but intended for the population of the city-state.

More recently, agrotechnology and agro-bio parks were established in Singapore itself, with surprisingly good results. Primarily located in the north-western districts of Chua Chu Kang and Lim Chu Kang, these highly productive farms mostly employ foreign labourers. They provide the city with a large variety of fresh leafy vegetables and some 30 per cent of its chicken eggs. Singapore's farm sector also supplies 15 per cent of the world market for cut orchids and nearly 20 per cent of the market for ornamental fish, for which it is the leading exporter.

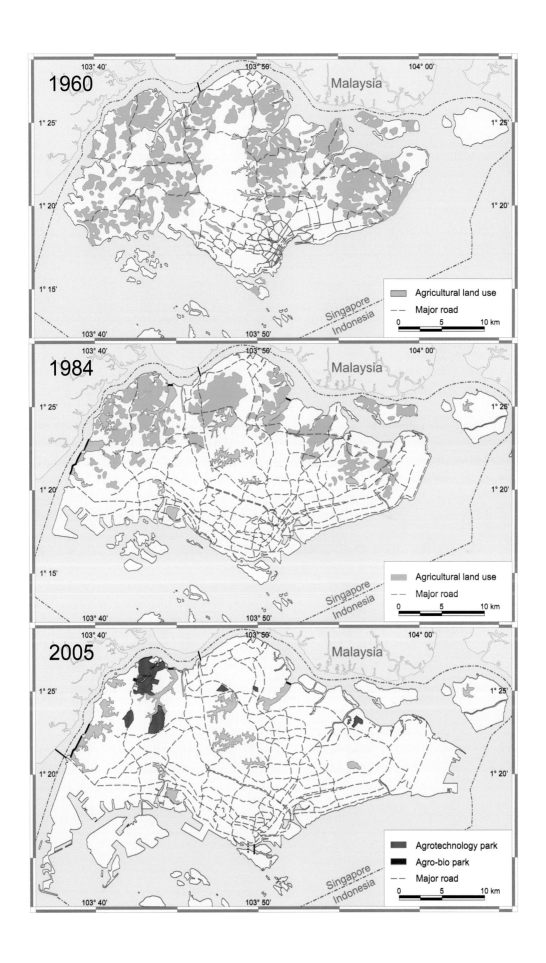

PLATE 16

Expanding and Consolidating Industry

From the early 1960s onwards, Singapore's industrial production grew very rapidly. Between 1961 and 1989, its contribution to Gross Domestic Product (GDP) grew from 12 per cent to 30 per cent. Over the same period, the GDP jumped from 2.1 to 55.3 billion Singapore dollars. Behind this expansion lay a vigorous industrialisation policy that granted large fiscal advantages to investors, local and foreign – multinationals in particular – in a context where local workers were offered intensive training and submitted to tight social control.

Singapore's remarkable industrial development could not, however, have been achieved without prior groundwork, literally. Before an industrial take-off could be generated, room had to be made for free trade zones and industrial estates. Jurong Industrial Estate, the most important, was inaugurated in 1961, and by 1965, the year of Singapore's foundation as an independent Republic, 151 factories were in place, all of them profiting from pioneer status and tax rebates. At that time, the developed part of the estate covered 400 hectares. Since then its expansion has never abated, although frequent adjustments and even industrial conversions had occurred throughout Singapore. These include the phasing out of the rubber industry, now flourishing where rubber is produced, in the Malay Peninsula, and the growth of the electronics industry.

In 1968 the government created the Jurong Town Corporation (JTC) and gave it a mandate to monitor the development of industrial estates, then in full expansion and relying on the implementation of intensive land reclamation. By the late 1980s, the JTC was managing twenty-four industrial estates occupying a total of 76 sq km throughout the island. These estates were home to more than 4,000 factories, half of them in Jurong alone. Among the other estates, the three largest ones, space wise – Kranji, Sungei Kadut and Woodlands – were located on the northern flank of the island. But the most populous industrial estates, where flatted factories proliferated, were dispersed on the margins of the urban core: Ayer Rajah, Ang Mo Kio and, especially, Kallang Basin.

Since then, industrial activities have been partly relocated in neighbouring Indonesia and Malaysia, while in Singapore itself, industrial employment has levelled off and even decreased. The manufacturing front has been stabilised, with higher value added industries favoured, and all sites located in peripheral areas, with Jurong's position as the pre-eminent industrial region being confirmed.

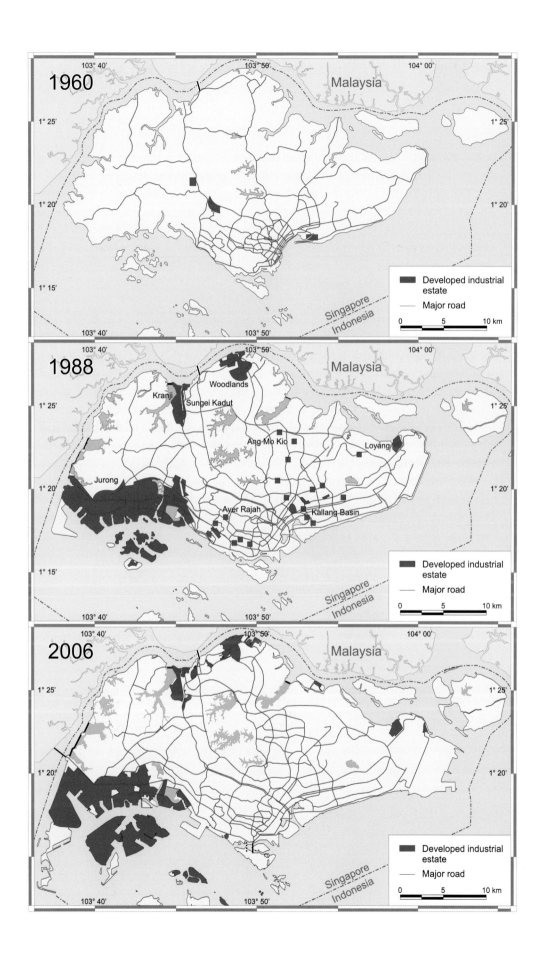

1960

1988

Kranji
Woodlands
Sungei Kadut
Ang Mo Kio
Loyang
Jurong
Ayer Rajah
Kallang Basin

2006

Malaysia

Developed industrial
estate
Major road

0   5   10 km

Singapore
Indonesia

PLATE 17

Jurong: From Mangrove to Industrial Estate

In the 1960s the overhaul of territory reached its greatest intensity in what was then the Jurong postal district, in the south-western part of the island. The area had extensive mangrove forests, and low hills whose slopes were largely devoted to agriculture. By the early 1980s the hills, some of them 30 to 40 metres high, had nearly all been levelled and the mangrove areas thoroughly filled. A single hill remained like a lone sentinel. Today, its slopes are occupied by a park and its crest by a water tower and an observation platform. These structures overlook the industrial estate and the consolidated, straightened and expanding coastline.

Few areas of the island have been so completely transformed. As the core of the initial industrial effort, the district has not only seen the establishment of hundreds of factories but also of a New Town, a residential estate created to house the workers. Its coast has become the new frontier for the expansion of the Singapore harbour, Jurong now equipped with its own terminal and various forms of ship-berthing facilities. These now reach into the Jurong Islands, the area of which has nearly quadrupled because the islands were merged into one very large and flat industrial platform, *the* Jurong Island. Until the late 1960s, the waters around these islands were still used for scuba diving. Today they share in the activities of the industrial estate and of the world's busiest harbour.

The "mainland" itself continues to expand along the Tuas peninsula in the direction of both Malaysia and Indonesia but still well within Singaporean territorial waters. That industrial expansion is in fact closely associated with a parallel development on the Malaysian side of the Johor Strait, to which Singapore has been linked financially and structurally by a bridge opened in 2000, commonly called the "second link" (see Plate 20).

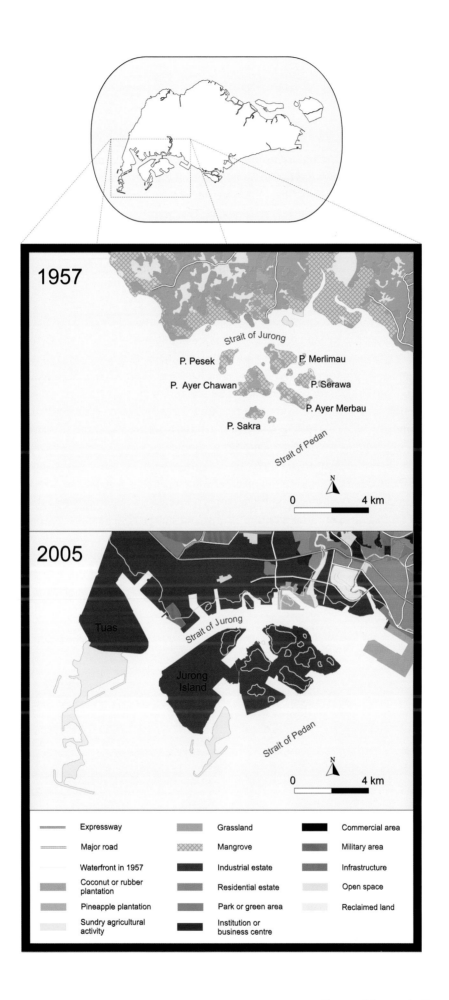

PLATE 18

Petroleum Islands

Starting in the 1960s, intensive construction of various types of industrial infrastructures occurred throughout the main island, to the point where these now occupy more than one tenth of its surface area. However, at least one sector achieved its own spectacular growth "*extra muros*", so to speak: the petroleum industry.

Initially needed for the rapid development of a city-state totally lacking in raw materials and reliant on manufacturing, the energy industry has become one of the key sectors in the Singapore export economy. At least one power station and all refineries and petrochemical installations have been stationed offshore, literally. Singapore's petroleum refining facilities – with an annual capacity of nearly 63 million tons – are primarily located on the newly assembled island of Jurong, at a relatively safe distance from the urban core and the major concentrations of population. At the end of the 1950s, several of the western and southern islands were inhabited by rural communities, predominantly Malay and earning their living at least in part from fishing. All residents have since been evacuated, and their houses, mosques, temples and cemeteries relocated to the main island. In their place, on islands often flattened and enlarged, or even fully constructed around coral reefs, stand towering fuel tanks, refineries and other industrial structures.

The powerful petroleum industry at one time accounted for as much as 40 per cent of the country's industrial production, but after peaking in 1982 this proportion has declined. The petroleum sector's share of the economy remains substantial, amounting to close to 30 per cent of industrial output, but perhaps more significant is the fact that commercial, technological and financial networks and flows linked to it have become crucial to the national economy. Singapore is not only a major refining and petrochemical centre but also the leading base in the region for offshore petroleum exploration and production.

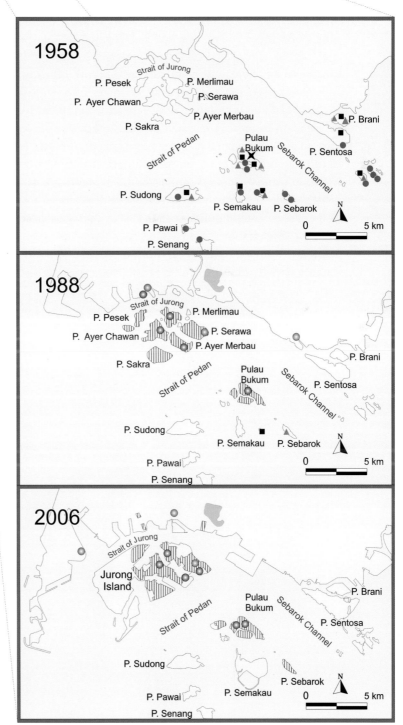

1958

Strait of Jurong
P. Pesek
P. Ayer Chawan
P. Merlimau
P. Serawa
P. Ayer Merbau
P. Sakra
P. Brani
P. Sentosa
Pulau Bukum
Strait of Pedan
Sebarok Channel
P. Sudong
P. Semakau
P. Sebarok
N
0   5 km
P. Pawai
P. Senang

1988

Strait of Jurong
P. Pesek
P. Ayer Chawan
P. Merlimau
P. Serawa
P. Ayer Merbau
P. Sakra
P. Brani
P. Sentosa
Strait of Pedan
Pulau Bukum
Sebarok Channel
P. Sudong
P. Semakau
P. Sebarok
N
0   5 km
P. Pawai
P. Senang

2006

Strait of Jurong
Jurong Island
Strait of Pedan
Pulau Bukum
Sebarok Channel
P. Brani
P. Sentosa
P. Sudong
P. Sebarok
N
P. Pawai
P. Semakau
0   5 km
P. Senang

■ School
▲ Mosque
● Muslim cemetery
✖ Oil depot
◉ Refinery
◉ Power station
▥ Petrochemical infrastructure

PLATE 19

Foreign Lands for Expansion: The Riau Islands

The requirements of industrial expansion, along with the thirst for water and the hunger for land to grow have led to a series of deals with Malaysia and Indonesia. In the case of Indonesia, the primary target area has been the neighbouring islands of the Riau Archipelago. These have become both a new industrial platform and a playground for Singaporean as well as other foreign tourists.

In fact the Riau islands are part of what has been known since the 1980s as the Singapore/Johor/Riau (SIJORI) growth triangle. Situated south and south-east of Singapore, these islands are heavily targeted by the overflow of Singaporean industrial capital. The island of Batam, located 20 km south-east of Singapore, plays the role of an offshore industrial platform, a site offering relatively inexpensive space and labour. Singapore based entrepreneurs have transferred some of their activities to the island and invested in new ventures. In typical Jurong fashion, Batam has been enlarged from its original size of 400 sq km to 715 sq km. This industrial frontier, located on Indonesian territory and relying on Indonesian labour, has spread into other islands, including Bintan, on the southern side of which the huge Batimindo Industrial Estate currently employs some 70,000 workers, most of them women. Singapore's overflow also reaches into the recreational sector, for example with the development of the Bintan International Tourist Resort on the northern shore of the island.

Both Batam and Bintan Islands are within easy reach for Singaporean entrepreneurs and tourists, by ferry – with more than 100 sailings per day from Singapore to Batam – and by plane.

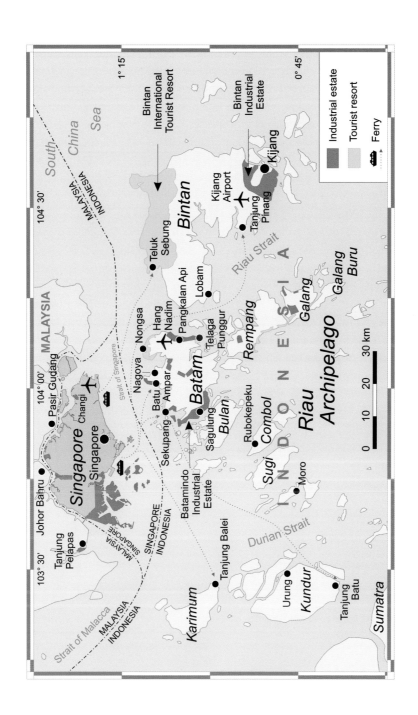

PLATE 20

Foreign Lands for Expansion: Johor

In the case of Malaysia, the southern part of Johor State has also since the early 1980s become the site of a number of industrial development ventures, largely financed by Singaporean capital. Officially regrouped in 2006 into the South Johor Development Region, perhaps better known as the Iskandar Development Region (IDR), this industrial frontier encompasses some 2,200 sq km, an area three times the size of Singapore. According to the 9th Malaysia plan (2006–2010), it is expected that by 2010 some one thousand factories and businesses, many linked to the information technology sector, will employ more than 120,000 workers. From the Malaysian point of view, this should limit the congestion which has been building up around Kuala Lumpur and the so-called Multimedia Super Corridor situated south of it.

The capital city of Johor State, located just across the causeway from Singapore, has become the command centre of this new growth region. J. B. as it is known familiarly, has itself been growing very rapidly, the population of its metropolitan region having doubled between 1991 and 2007, to about 900,000 inhabitants. This is attributable to its role both as capital of Johor State and of the IDR, and also as receiving centre for a number of additional Singaporean activities, which include recreation, shopping and investment in housing.

Apart from a number of industrial parks expanding all over the interior of the Iskandar region, three major harbour centres are fast developing on the shores of the Johor Strait. Located at its western extremity, the most important of the three is Tanjung Pelapas harbour. Backed by its own industrial park, it is already competing with Singapore's Tanjung Pagar terminal for container handling. Finally, north of J. B., located within the IDR, Senai Airport has until recently been expanding rapidly, thanks to its function as a hub for Air Asia, a successful Malaysian budget airline.

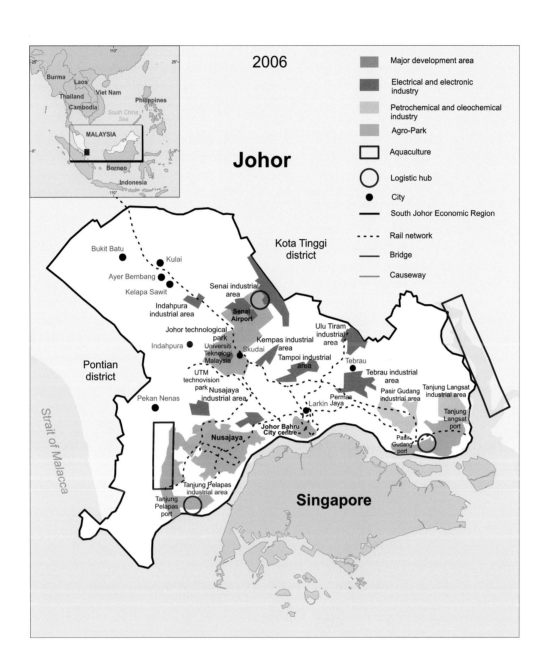

2006

Johor

Legend	
■	Major development area
■	Electrical and electronic industry
■	Petrochemical and oleochemical industry
■	Agro-Park
▭	Aquaculture
◯	Logistic hub
●	City
—	South Johor Economic Region
---	Rail network
—	Bridge
—	Causeway

Burma
Laos
Thailand
Viet Nam
Cambodia
Philippines
South China Sea
MALAYSIA
Borneo
Indonesia

Bukit Batu
Kulai
Ayer Bembang
Kelapa Sawit
Indahpura industrial area
Johor technological park
Indahpura
Universiti Teknologi Malaysia
Skudai
UTM technovision park
Nusajaya industrial area
Pekan Nenas
Nusajaya

Kota Tinggi district

Senai industrial area
Senai Airport
Kempas industrial area
Tampoi industrial area
Ulu Tiram industrial area
Tebrau
Tebrau industrial area
Pasir Gudang industrial area
Tanjung Langsat industrial area
Tanjung Langsat port
Permas Jaya
Larkin
Johor Bahru City centre
Pasir Gudang port

Pontian district

Strait of Malacca

Tanjung Pelapas industrial area
Tanjung Pelapas port

Singapore

PLATE 21

Foreign Lands for Expansion: The World

Singapore's economic expansion has of course gone well beyond the shores of immediate neighbouring lands. Besides its rather impressive network of diplomatic missions – impressive at least for a country of its size – besides also the remarkable network of its "ambassador" airline (see Plate 26), the city-state's global reach manifests itself in a number of additional ways.

For example Singapore Telecom, better known as SingTel and admittedly the largest Singapore based corporation, has been expanding very aggressively during recent years, particularly within Asia. In 2006, Temasek Holdings, the Singapore government's financial arm established in 1974, still held 63 per cent of SingTel's shares.

Numerous other government linked companies (GLC), as they are known locally, can also count on the government to help them expand globally. This can be achieved through International Enterprise Singapore, an offshoot of the former Singapore Trade Developmenet Board. Although International Enterprise, also known as Intelligent Enterprise, has been privatised and is not officially recognised as a GLC, it definitely acts as one. It maintains a network of representative offices throughout the world, just like SingTel, which helps link Singapore enterprises – the so-called Singapore Inc. – doing business with international partners, as well as advises those among the latter who want to invest in Singapore. Singaporean investments are spread throughout the world, with a major focus in Southeast Asia and in two of the planet's leading economies, the USA and China.

The Port of Singapore Authority also counts among Singaporean major global players. Besides operating the six terminals of Singapore harbour, the world's busiest, in 2006 it also operated terminals located in fifteen additional countries.

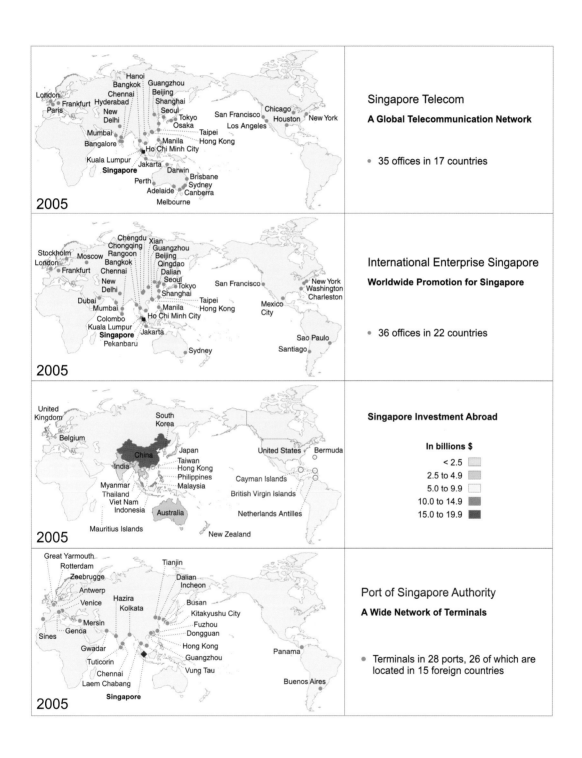

Singapore Telecom

A Global Telecommunication Network

- 35 offices in 17 countries

International Enterprise Singapore

Worldwide Promotion for Singapore

- 36 offices in 22 countries

Singapore Investment Abroad

In billions $

< 2.5	
2.5 to 4.9	
5.0 to 9.9	
10.0 to 14.9	
15.0 to 19.9	

Port of Singapore Authority

A Wide Network of Terminals

- Terminals in 28 ports, 26 of which are located in 15 foreign countries

PLATE 22

Making Way for Cars

The spatial expansion of the industrial estates and of residential areas, particularly New Towns, added to the growing purchasing power of Singaporeans, was accompanied by a steady rise in the number of motor vehicles on the island and a phenomenal improvement of its transport infrastructure. The constant expansion of the road network and particularly of expressways represents one of the most noticeable forms of territorial restructuring – some might say deconstructing – the island has undergone. The Bukit Timah Expressway, a six-lane dual carriageway completed in the 1980s, east of the still operational Bukit Timah Road, provides a good example.

The continuous increase in the number of cars circulating on the island's road network is occurring in the face of a series of disincentives decreed by the government. These include some of the highest car prices in the world (all cars are imported); very high taxes for ownership itself, including an expensive Certificate of Entitlement (or COE); high costs for fuel and parking; repeated increases in the levies collected for access, during peak hours, to the downtown core and to a number of expressways; and strict enforcement of traffic rules. But the resulting paradox is only apparent. For both the very entrepreneurially minded government as well as the citizens, particularly those belonging to the middle and upper classes, seem to cope well with this evolving situation. Notwithstanding the slowly increasing congestion of the once famously smooth city-state traffic, Singaporeans continue to buy cars and to bid for the COE, while the government continues to contract out numerous and lucrative road construction projects. For those who cannot afford car ownership and use, there is the equally expanding and improving public transport system and a large fleet of taxis providing an efficient and relatively cheap service.

Year	1970	1988	2006
Cars	150,000	240,000	474,700
Motor vehicles	260,000	500,000	799,400
Surfaced roads in km	1,300	2,700	8,000
Expressways in km	40	90	150

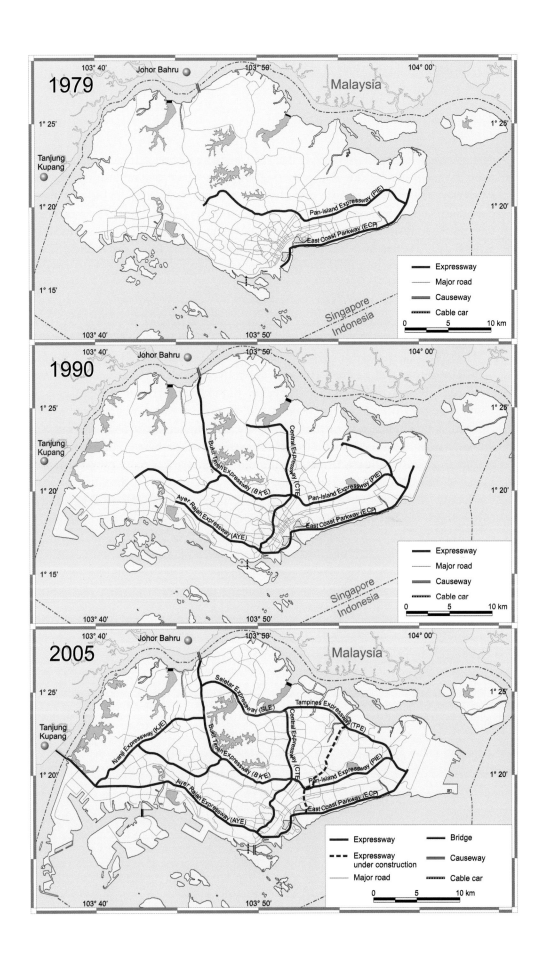

PLATE 23

Transporting Workers

A single track metre gauge railway line running from Keppel Railway Station in downtown Singapore to the causeway crossing the Johor Strait was built in 1923, replacing a line laid down 20 years earlier and further to the east. Along with the antiquated yet charming Keppel Station, it actually belongs to Malaysia. Apart from an extension to the Jurong Industrial Estate, constructed in the early 1960s and since removed, this railway line has hardly been improved and remains little used, except by a few daily freight trains and two or three short passenger trains running daily between Singapore and Kuala Lumpur.

However, beginning in the late 1980s, an urban rail network was put into place within Singapore Island, and has since expanded at record pace. The Mass Rapid Transit (MRT) system's first five stations opened in November 1987. Before the end of 1990, 41 stations and 67 km of rail line were operational. By 2005, the number of MRT stations had reached 105 and the network covered nearly 110 km, with an additional 31 km track handling so-called Light Rapid Transit (LRT) trains. Since 1999, three LRT lines have been opened. Of the three much more extensive MRT lines currently operational, one of them traverses the southern part of the island, linking the industrial south-west with Changi Airport in the south-east and passing through the urban core. Another line, also longitudinal, links the core with the increasingly populous north-east of the island, where two LRT lines redistribute the commuters. Called the North South line, the third MRT line could be more aptly named the Outer Circle line as it links, through a big loop, the aforementioned lines with the North of the island. The MRT network is still undergoing expansion, with an Inner Circle line due to open in 2010 and three additional lines planned over the next 20 years. Moreover, an efficient bus service connects major terminals around the island, and is well integrated with the train network, ensuring that public transport will continue to offer a strong alternative to private car ownership.

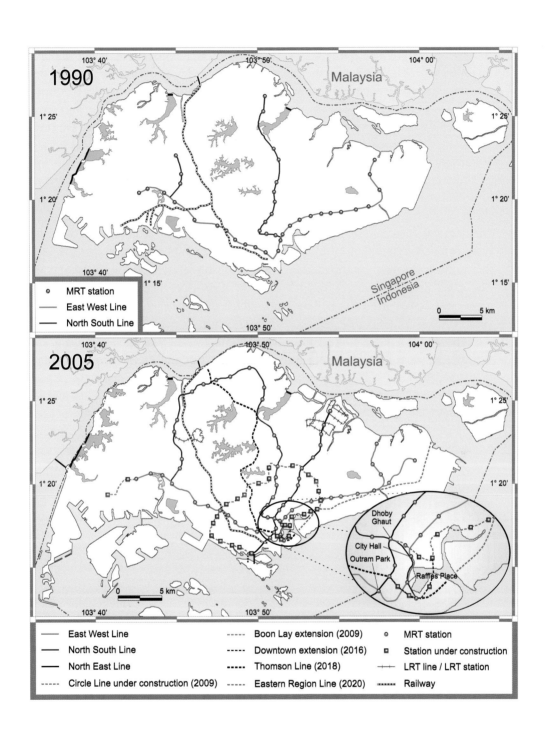

PLATE 24

Doors Wide Open to the World

In 1960, Singapore's then unique seaport terminal, Keppel Harbour, handled 12 million tons of cargo. In 1989, the volume had reached 173 million tons, with petroleum accounting for nearly half of the total. That year, 39,000 ships visited its five terminals and 15 km of docks, all well serviced by 600 sq km of port waters, the surface of the latter having doubled since 1960. This made Singapore the world's busiest port, and it has since maintained its rank as the world's leading maritime trade centre with, in 2006, some 129,000 ships stopping in its port waters and more than 440 million tons of cargo handled by its six terminals. More than half of that cargo was in the form of containers, while most of the bulk cargo was oil. On the south and south-west shore of the island, five terminals are lined up – Tanjong Pagar, Brani, Keppel, Pasir Panjang and Jurong – with port facilities extending up to Tuas and into the islands lying offshore. The sixth terminal is on the northern shore of the island, next to the Sembawang shipyard established in 1968 on the site of the former British naval base. The giant Brani terminal was opened in the 1990s on the island bearing the same name, just across from Keppel Harbour, which remains the centrepiece of the whole system.

The network of terminals administered by the Port of Singapore Authority extends worldwide, since PSA manages more than twenty terminals spread around the world, in fifteen countries. This represents another form of the expansion of Singapore, which, beyond its dynamism as a maritime trade centre, has developed an equally competitive air transport function. The island hosts three military airports (Tengah, Sembawang and Paya Lebar), and two civil ones (Seletar and Changi) covering in total some 20 sq km, most of this being the domain of the giant and still expanding Changi airport. The military airbases as well as the naval bases have themselves gone through a number of relocations. For example, in the early 1970s, the Singapore navy's main base was on Brani Island. By the mid-1990s it was partially relocated on the Tuas peninsula. In 2004, a larger site was added off the Changi coast, and the Brani base closed in 2000. Overall, military facilities occupy a substantial proportion of the national territory.

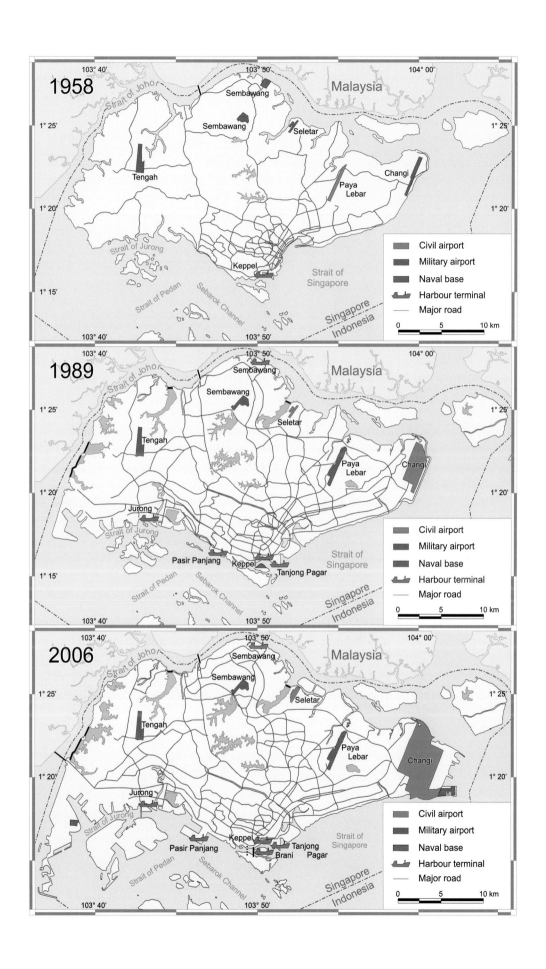

PLATE 25

Changi: An Airport in the Sea

Like much of Singapore's industrial infrastructure, Changi airport, Southeast Asia's leading air transport centre, sits on reclaimed land. In 1958, when Britain's military installations were still operational, the island had two civil airports, in Kallang and Paya Lebar, and ten military bases – occupying in total 10 per cent of the surface area of the island. Four of the military bases had runways. Following the 1968–1971 British military withdrawal, the Singapore Armed Forces inherited part of the installations, including the Seletar air base, which was handed over to the Civil Aviation Authority, and the Tengah air base. Kallang airport was closed down, but Paya Lebar was maintained and eventually ceded to the military. In July 1981, passenger traffic was transferred from Paya Lebar to Changi. This huge airport had just been completed on the site of a former military runway, laid out in 1943 during the Japanese Occupation. By 1981, it had been thoroughly transformed and extended on reclaimed land. From then on its expansion has been steady. Singapore airport now operates two runways, each four kilometres long, and two full-blown terminals to which a so-called budget terminal, for budget airlines, was added in 2006. A third "standard" terminal, of a size equivalent to that of the first two, is to be opened in 2008, perhaps sharing with the Singapore Air Force what is in fact a third runway, already used by the SAF. So far, Changi has gained 13 sq km on the sea.

In the late 1950s and in fact well into the 1970s, this eastern tip of Singapore island was primarily rural; the land was mainly used for agriculture, and several Malay fishing villages dotted the shoreline. Now, as this shoreline continues to expand seaward, the airport surrounds itself, on the inland side, with vast industrial and trading installations, with ample land kept for parks and green areas. Perhaps even more than the Singapore harbour facilities, Changi airport – or Airtropolis according to the Singapore government jargon – symbolises the small city-state's close ties to the world. Linked to 183 cities in 57 countries, it handled in 2006 some 214,000 aircraft movements and more than 35 million passengers.

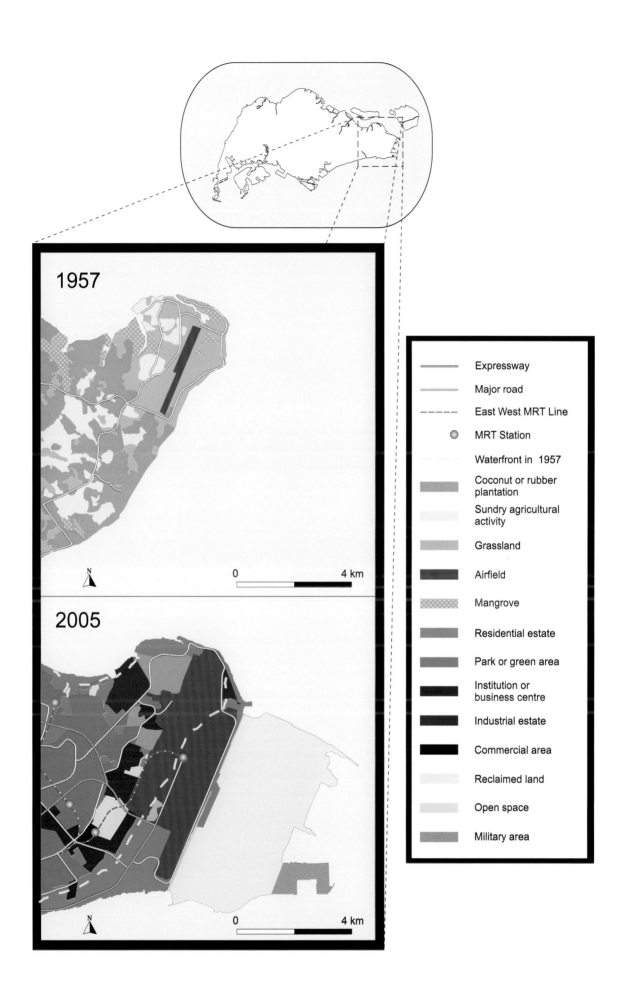

1957

2005

Expressway

Major road

East West MRT Line

MRT Station

Waterfront in 1957

Coconut or rubber plantation

Sundry agricultural activity

Grassland

Airfield

Mangrove

Residential estate

Park or green area

Institution or business centre

Industrial estate

Commercial area

Reclaimed land

Open space

Military area

PLATE 26

SIA: A World Class Airline

In 1965, when Singapore separated from Malaysia, the two countries continued to operate jointly Malaysia-Singapore Airlines. When this joint partnership was terminated in 1972, two airlines were formed: Singapore Airlines (SIA) and Malaysian Airlines System (MAS), the "system" having since been dropped. Both have become quite successful, SIA in particular. In 2006, the SIA network, together with that of Silk Air, its partner airline which limits its services to the regional market, extended to over 90 destinations in some 30 countries.

SIA is largely recognised as one of the world's best and also one of the most successful financially. It benefits from the fact that it does not need, as do many other airlines, to service isolated and less lucrative national markets. It is strictly an international airline, its network reflecting to a large extent the global reach of Singapore Inc. The latter is largely present in industrial countries, but has yet to make a breakthrough in Latin America and in much of Africa.

Another one of SIA's assets lies with the quality and youth of its fleet of aircraft and its constant opening of new routes, such as, in 2004, non-stop flights from Singapore to Los Angeles and to New York, in both cases a world's first. Although SIA has been privatised, the Singapore government still holds a majority of its shares. And, similar to many GLCs, it is constantly expanding by diversifying its assets, including through the purchase of shares in other airlines, such as Virgin and Indian Airlines.

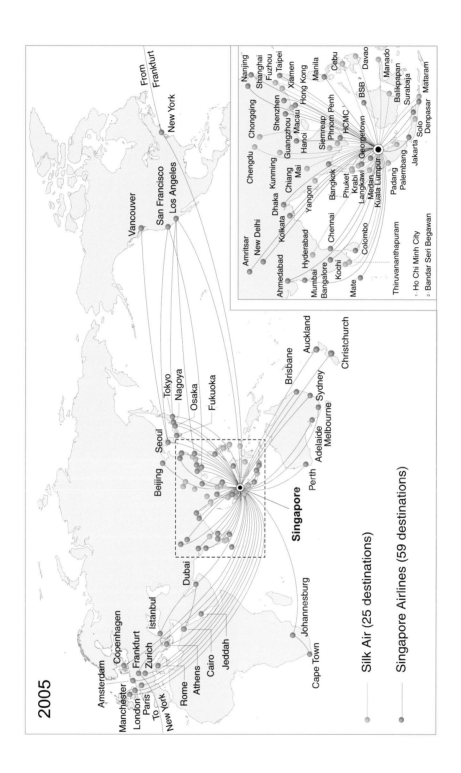

2005

Silk Air (25 destinations)

Singapore Airlines (59 destinations)

5
Services, Control and Entertainment

The rationale for the Singapore government's approach to nation-building has always been and continues to be the nurturing of the growth of a Singaporean national identity among the population, which will surmount all the chauvinistic and particularistic pulls of the Chinese, Malay, or Indian identities of the various groups on the island. — Jon S.T. Quah, 1990, p. 45

The possibly dark side of this policy is the management and control of the internal environment which the PAP government claims are necessary for the successful management of the external environment. — Linda Y. C. Lim, 1990, p. 135

The relocation of large numbers of people, largely achieved through the development of New Towns, is accompanied by the construction of a new environment, to which the new arrivals must adapt. This concerns everything from schools and temples, to burial arrangements, to social and political monitoring institutions such as community centres and, finally, to recreational facilities. Such reshufflings illustrate the extent to which the entire Singapore living environment is constantly being redefined. They also suggest the degree to which the population is at the disposal of the perpetual development process and the tight control that it necessitates.

PLATE 27

Places to Pray

Since the late 1950s, the number of places of worship, whether temples, mosques or churches, has increased substantially, although no faster than the overall population. But even when the population is now more widely distributed throughout the island, such "places to pray" appear less dispersed. This is due to two factors: the removal of large numbers of families from several peripheral regions, some of which have been completely emptied, and the formation of New Towns, which constitute large population nuclei. More fundamentally, the evolution in the number of places of worship, depending on the religions of the dominant communities, has been quite different. For example, by 1988, following expropriations, nearly 90 of the more than 200 Taoist temples existing in 1958 had disappeared, although several of these so-called "Chinese" temples, then frowned upon by the authorities, were reincarnated as Buddhist temples. During that same period, Malay and Indian communities, no less subject to expropriations and resettlement, nonetheless witnessed a substantial increase in the number of mosques and temples. But this growth in the number of Buddhist, Muslim, Hindu or even Sikh places of worship appeared much less striking than that of Christian churches, which increased in number from 32 to 127. This trend was confirmed between 1988 and 2005, when the number of mosques and Hindu and Buddhist temples decreased, but the number of churches nearly doubled from 127 to 239. The same period brought a reinvigoration of Taoism along with Chinese cultural pride.

Places of worship	1958	1988	2005
Taoist temples	215	127	163
Mosques	76	99	71
Hindu temples	13	38	26
Churches	32	127	239
Buddhist temples	7	75	62
Other			
Sikh temples		9	7
Synagogues		1	2
TOTAL	343	476	570

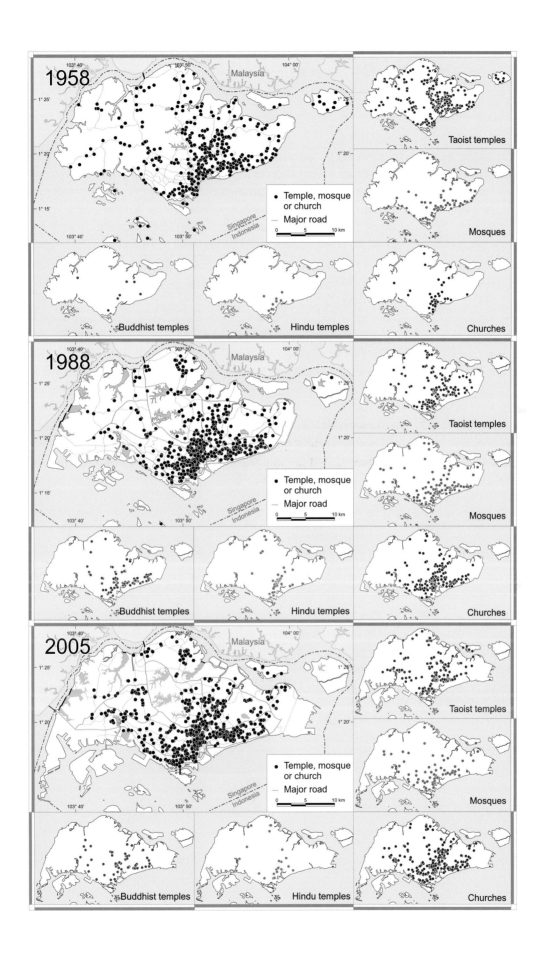

PLATE 28

Places for Burial

The nature and location of burial grounds as well as sites for ancestor worship are important in most cultures and exceptionally so with the Chinese. Yet Singaporean cemeteries have also been the object of curtailment and massive transfers. Their total number, which in 1958 stood at 113, had been reduced to 64 in 1988 and 25 by 2005. Exhumations followed by relocations have been most frequent in the central urban area and in the peripheral islands, affecting Chinese and Muslim cemeteries in particular. Although reliance on columbaria and crematoria located in the more densely populated areas is spreading rapidly, a sector covering several hectares in the western part of the island has nevertheless been earmarked for cemeteries. This burial reserve ground in the nearly empty Western Water Catchment district is set among low rolling hills and forms one of the most harmonious landscapes on the island. By 1988, a dozen cemeteries had already been established in the area, at the disposal of those who wished and could afford to give their dead a traditional burial, whether following Chinese, Muslim, Hindu, Buddhist, Jew, Parsi, Bahai or Christian rites. Since then, the overall number of cemeteries has been further reduced, and those that remain are even more closely grouped.

Cemeteries	1958	1988	2005
Chinese	54	25	8
Muslim	47	20	8
Hindu	3	3	2
Christian	3	7	3
Others	6	9	4
TOTAL	113	64	25
Columbaria and Crematoria	0	5	16

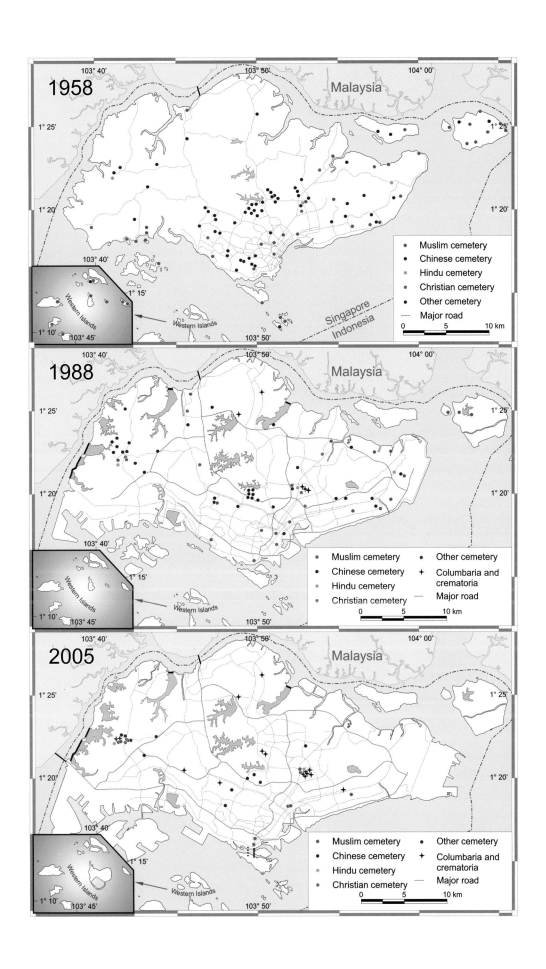

PLATE 29

Places to Study

Somewhat ambivalent on religious matters, the State's policy on the preferred language for education is clear: the ideal lies in uniformity. Chinese, Malay, Tamil, and English are all recognised as official languages with Malay having the added status of national language, but English has become the primary medium throughout the educational system. In 1965, schools were identified in ethno-linguistic or religious terms, but such designations no longer exist. Since independence in 1965, the Singapore government's commitment to education has never abated. Even with the very substantial growth of the resources at its disposal, it has continuously allocated at least 10 per cent of the national budget to the education sector, and nearly 25 per cent during the 1970s. School construction has been quite active.

All levels and denominations included, there were 235 schools in 1965 and 725 in 1990, and the literacy rate climbed from 52 per cent (in 1957) to 90 per cent in 1990 and 95 per cent in 2005. The geographical distribution of primary and secondary schools now follows closely that of the New Towns. The case of vocational training schools appears particularly interesting. They proliferated during the 1970s and 1980s, mostly in the urban core. Since the early 1990s, their number has been greatly reduced, while the institutions of higher learning, including polytechnics, have steadily increased. Several of these, including the National University, have been regrouped on its western flank, halfway between the city and the Jurong Industrial Estate, while more recently others have been established at the very core of the city.

Schools	1966	1990	2005
Chinese schools	107	0	0
Malay schools	37	0	0
Tamil schools	41	0	0
English schools	12	0	0
Primary and secondary schools		316	357
Institutions of higher learning	6	8	16
Other schools	79	405	130
TOTAL	282	729	503

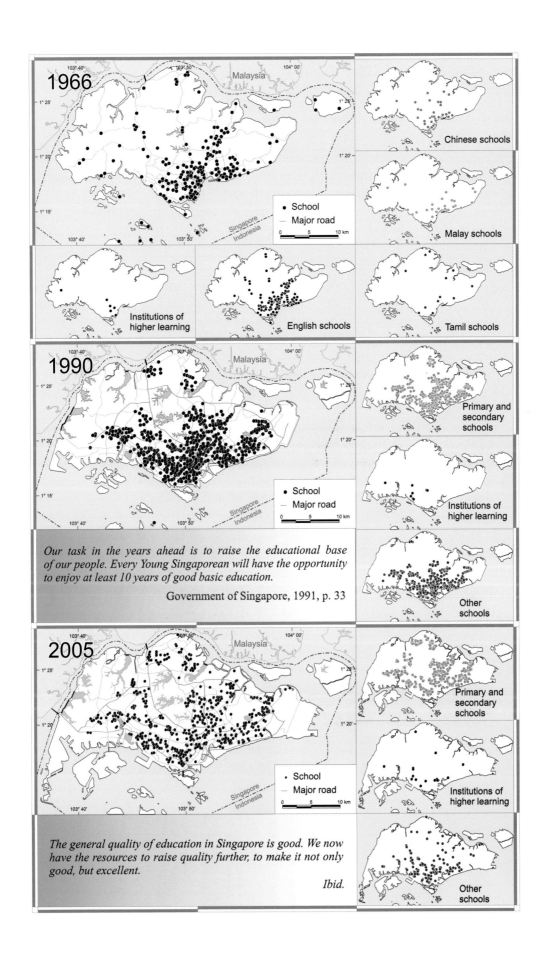

1966

Chinese schools

Malay schools

Institutions of
higher learning

English schools

Tamil schools

- School
— Major road
0   5   10 km

1990

Primary and
secondary
schools

Institutions of
higher learning

Other
schools

- School
— Major road
0   5   10 km

*Our task in the years ahead is to raise the educational base
of our people. Every Young Singaporean will have the opportunity
to enjoy at least 10 years of good basic education.*

Government of Singapore, 1991, p. 33

2005

Primary and
secondary
schools

Institutions of
higher learning

Other
schools

- School
— Major road
0   5   10 km

*The general quality of education in Singapore is good. We now
have the resources to raise quality further, to make it not only
good, but excellent.*

Ibid.

PLATE 30

Places for Recreation

Towards the end of the 1950s, forested areas and natural beaches, particularly in the outer islands, were among the favourite recreational areas. As access to this "wilderness" was progressively curtailed by the depletion of the natural forest and the industrialisation of the shoreline, enormous energy went into the development of parks, beaches, stadiums and swimming pool complexes – in principle, each New Town has at its disposal an Olympic size pool – and other sport facilities. (Parks have been discussed above in connection with the evolution of the Garden City; see Plate 8.)

To these green parks could be added numerous theme parks – not represented here – that have sprung up in several areas. These include the Jurong Bird Park, and the extensive Zoological Garden near the Upper Seletar Reservoir. Equally noticeable, the establishment of specialised recreation sites has brought about the thorough transformation of substantial pieces of land. This is the case, notably, of Pulau Sentosa, the "island of tranquility". Located a short distance from the urban core, just beyond Pulau Brani, it is often referred to, and for good reason, as the Disneyland of Singapore. This island was one of the choice pieces in the land bank ceded to the Singapore government by the British military following their 1968 to 1971 withdrawal. Since then, it has been extended and equipped to host a wide range of recreational facilities, including theme parks, museums, resort-type hotels, marinas, beaches largely fabricated with imported sand and cement boulders made to look like natural ones, and three very prominent golf courses. The success of Pulau Sentosa, which can be reached by ferry, cable car or over a causeway, has been such that Pulau Ubin, in the Strait of Johor, is to be transformed into another type of recreation platform.

As for golf courses, which attract rich tourists as well as rich Singaporeans, they now number 23 – doubtless with more to come – occupying nearly 17 sq km or more than 2 per cent of the national territory, an astonishing proportion for a land hungry city-state.

Places for recreation	1958	1988	2005
Golf courses	2	13	23
Public swimming pools/complexes	3	23	22
Stadiums	0	13	17

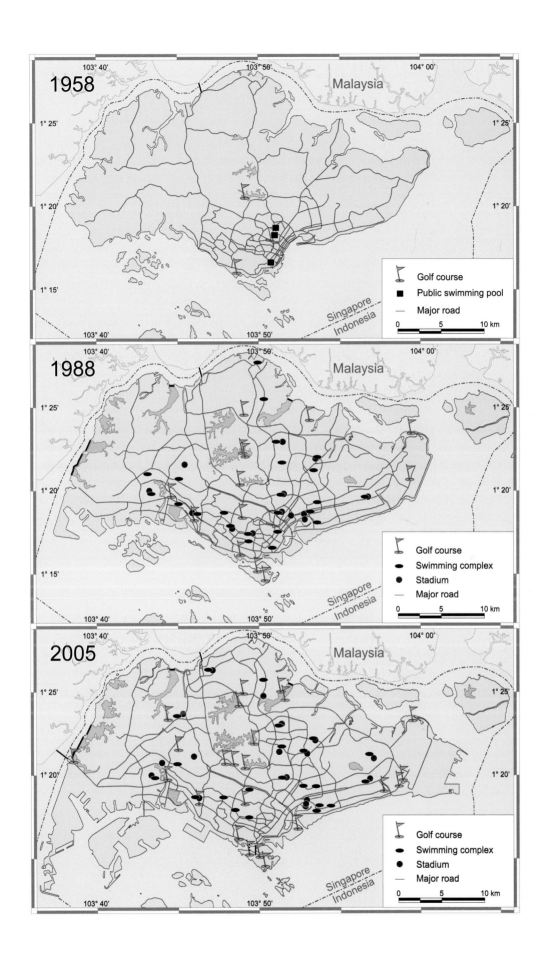

PLATE 31

Rallying Points

In the mid-1950s there were around 20 Community Centres in Singapore, with most of them situated in the central urban area. Shortly after achieving power in 1959, the People's Action Party (PAP) set about increasing their number and expanding their functions, until then predominantly recreational. The task was assigned to the People's Association, created in 1960. Since then, the association has played a crucial role in the population's cultural, social and political nurturing. The latter mandate appeared dominant during the 1960s, the Centres essentially fulfilling the role of local branch offices or rallying points for the ruling party. Ordinary citizens visiting them for essential services were also exposed to a political message.

Combined with their broad geographical spread, the Centres' proliferation ensured a near total coverage of the territory, whether urban or rural, including, then, the small islands. Today, their socio-cultural function appears prevalent once again, people having access to a broad range of educational and recreational resources, to which are added nursery and kindergarten services.

The location of Community Centres has evolved along with the redistribution of population. Many have been closed down or regrouped, and new ones established. As a result, the distribution pattern of the 112 centres still existing in 2005 is quite different from that of 1968, when the number stood at 181. The reduction in their numbers may be an indication that their social and political monitoring function has become less important.

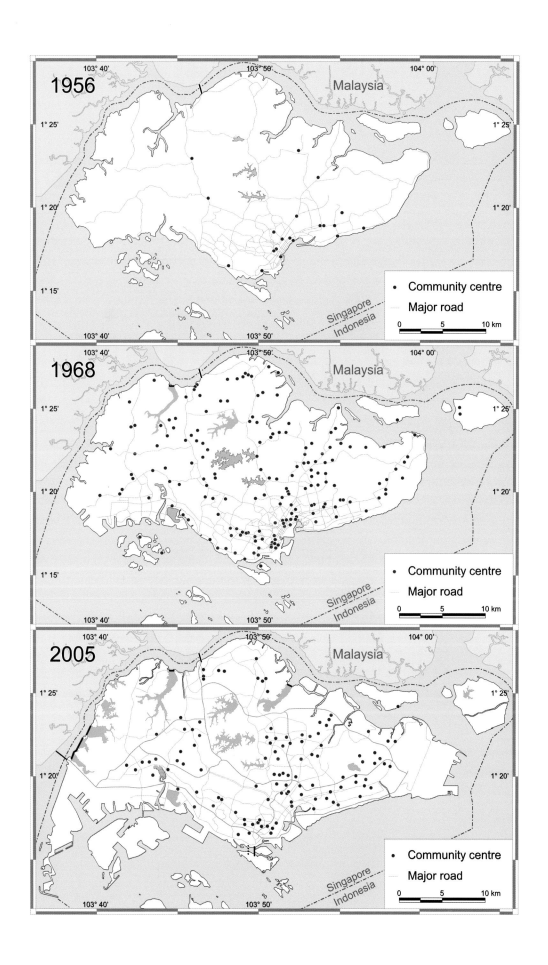

PLATE 32

The Tourist Trail: Orchard Road

In 1959, Singapore was an unusual destination for the traveller, and its tourism infrastructure, apart from a few grand and exotic hotels such as the Raffles or the Goodwood Park, was poorly developed. The fifty-odd hotels, half of which were operating without a licence, offered a total of about 1,000 rooms, and fewer than 100,000 foreigners visited Singapore annually. However, the transformations to the urban and island wide landscape and the improvement of transport infrastructure were followed by tourist promotion campaigns and the construction of luxury hotels. As a result, some thirty years later, the city-state had nearly 150 licensed hotels, with the seventy largest ones offering together a total of 25,000 rooms.

Tourism had become big business and the construction of huge luxury hotels almost a routine operation. At the end of 1989, there were twenty-six hotels with 400 rooms or more. Along with skyscrapers bordering the Singapore River, hotel towers are now a characteristic feature of Singapore's urban profile. To make room for them and for the numerous shopping plazas which delight tourists and foreign residents and perhaps even more the Singaporean residents, a major avenue and its surroundings were redesigned. Orchard Road – often but somewhat inappropriately referred to as the Singaporean "Champs-Élysées" – and its extension towards Marina Bay have been made into a kind of shopping mall cum tourist trail. By itself alone, that five kilometre trail hosts more than fifty hotels. Twenty-five of them are located along Orchard Road or in its immediate vicinity and they boast a total of more than 10,000 rooms.

To accommodate these hotels and the equally ubiquitous and even more extended shopping plazas, the road network has been thoroughly redesigned, which is another routine operation in contemporary Singapore.

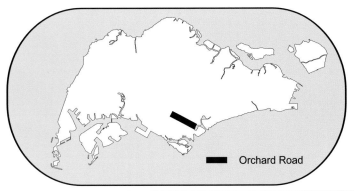

Orchard Road

1959

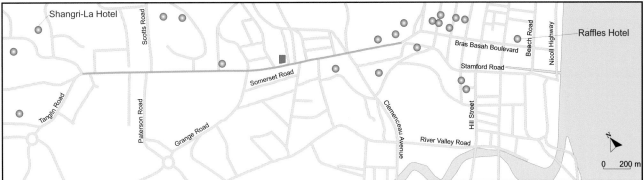

1990

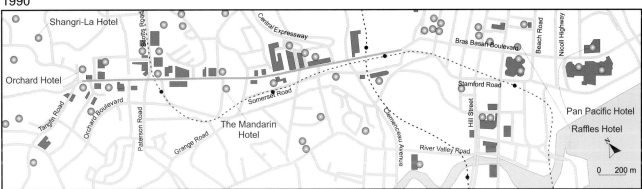

2005

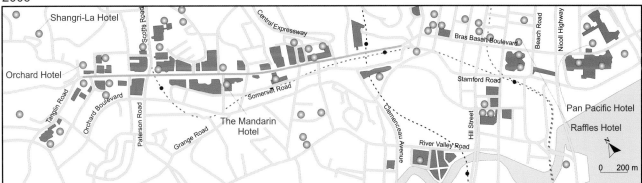

—— Orchard Road	------- East West MRT Line	
—— Road	------- North South MRT Line	
▬ Shopping Plaza	------- North East MRT Line	
◉ Hotel	• MRT Station	

6

The Perpetual Production of Territory in Singapore

Those who plan do better than those who do not plan even though they rarely stick to their plan. — Winston Churchill

The Master Plan is the statutory land use plan which guides Singapore's development in the medium term, over the next 10 to 15 years. It is reviewed once every five years, and translates the broad long-term strategies as set out in the Concept Plan into detailed implementable plans for Singapore. It shows the permissible land use and density for every parcel of land in Singapore. — Urban Redevelopment Authority, Master Plan 2003 website

It is essential to understand that space precedes territory. ... Space represents the "original prison", territory is the prison that men give themselves. — Translated from Raffestin, 1980, p. 129

Proposed as early as 1974 by the French philosopher, Henri Lefebvre, the concept of production of space, physical and social, became popular, even fashionable among geographers, particularly after his work was translated into English in 1994. Less known but perhaps more fundamental were contributions to the debate on the issue by Raffestin and Bresso (1979) and Raffestin (1980), which made a distinction between space and territory. Territory, they suggested, is space in which labour has been invested, and territoriality is the relation that people have with space in which they have invested labour as well as emotions. Redefining and monitoring territoriality is therefore an ultimate form of control.

By constantly "replanning" the rules of access to space, the Singaporean State is thus redefining territoriality, even in its minute details. It is thus able to consolidate its control over civil society to an extent rarely known in history.

PLATE 33

From Master Plan to Revised Model: 1958 to 2003

The tendency to plan territorial functions and to appeal to the population to adapt to them was already implicit when the First Master Plan was adopted in 1958, after several years of preparation. It was meant to be the basic reference for planning Singapore's development until 1972. Well before that date, however, the political conditions necessary for its implementation were compromised. It was subsequently revised on a five-year basis, and the 1975, 1980 and 1985 versions were substantially different from the original. Another document, the Comprehensive Long Range Development Plan or Concept Plan, which was first drafted in 1967 and bore the imprint of the leaders of the newly independent republic, gradually superseded the Master Plan. Adopted in 1970, it defined the real planning goals to be pursued until 1992. Less rigid and more vague than the Master Plan, the Concept Plan still revealed clearly the futuristic views of the Singapore planners and their firm resolution to continue to shape the territory and its occupants to fit their Model-State.

The 1991 Master Plan, derived from the Concept Plan as revised in 1991, is substantially different from its 1958 predecessor. It is much more detailed and at the same time more ambitious, particularly regarding land reclamation, industrial development and population redistribution. Even if the Concept Plan was revised again in 2001 and in 2005, the current Master Plan adopted in 2003 – replacing one adopted in 1998 – follows the lead of the 1991 version, but is even more detailed. Beyond this Master Plan, which can be consulted on the Urban Redevelopment Authority website, more specific plans, whether thematic or local, are also made available to the public. In this way Singaporeans can, in principle, learn what is likely to happen to any given piece of land or block of flats on the island and make appropriate personal financial plans. There lies one of the more paradoxical elements of citizen participation in Singapore's permanent transformation. Individuals can share or attempt to share in the financial "rewards" of constant redevelopment, but they nevertheless are not generally requested nor expected to contribute to the decision making process.

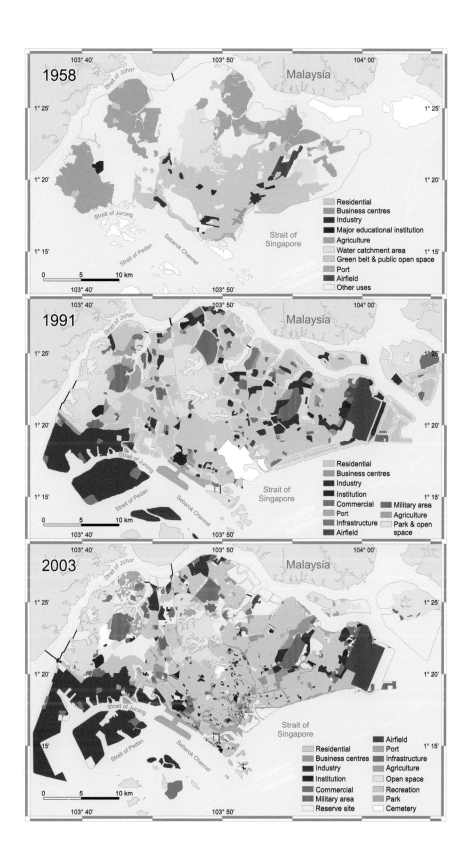

PLATE 34

Land Use in 2005

When compared to the 2003 Master Plan map (see Plate 33), the 2005 Land Use map reveals the extraordinary degree to which the actual land use throughout the country conforms to the plan. However, the land use map is more revealing on certain issues. One of the more evident issues concerns the amount of land that is *de facto* allocated to military use. To the substantial areas utilised by the major air bases – starting from the western side of the island, Tengah, Sembawang, Paya Lebar – must be added several other locations across the island, in particular much of the very large Western Water Catchment district.

At least three additional features are illustrated somewhat more clearly: first, the relative importance of land devoted to green spaces, whether categorised as recreation land, park or wooded area; second, the manner in which residential areas have nearly become a single contiguous mass centred on the hilly and wooded Bukit Timah Nature Reserve and, third, the stages of land reclamation, distinguishing between recently reclaimed land and what was still to come.

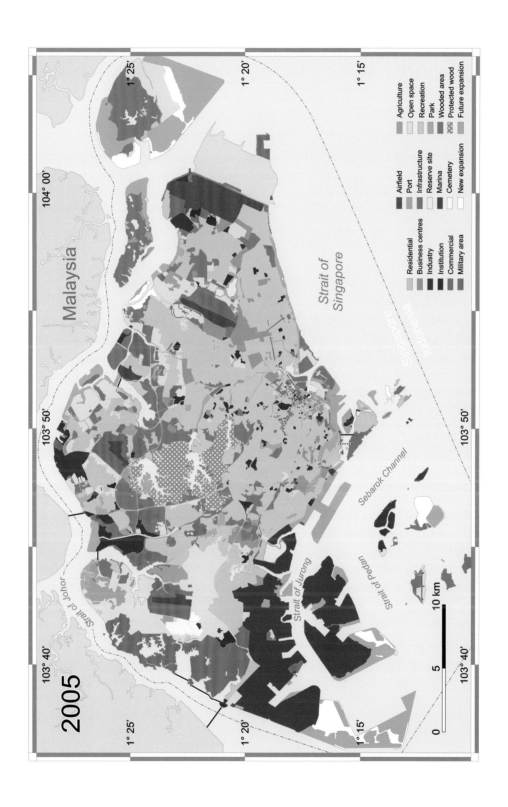

Conclusion: The Moveable Stage

There is much more to the transformations of the territory of Singapore than can be shown here. First, the discussion has only dealt with a relatively small number of topics, with many other potentially revealing ones being left aside. These include, for example, the "sedentarisation" of food hawkers and the transformation of hawker centres into so-called food courts, and the island-wide redistribution and proliferation of shopping plazas, although the plate devoted to the Orchard road area (no. 32) does provide a good illustration. Second, changing distributions have only been illustrated on a country-wide scale. It is quite obvious, as suggested in the introduction, that the same changes are occurring on a more local scale, at the level of the district, the neighbourhood, such as Chinatown, or the street, such as Bugis street. At this level photographs taken at different points in time would illustrate the magnitude of the territorial transformations. Third, data are not available to deal with a particularly sensitive issue that is part and parcel of the Singaporean permanent transformation – the function and distribution of foreign workers in the country. Fourth, on other sensitive issues, such as the already mentioned topic of the "construction" of electoral district maps, we chose not to deal with it.

The book then does not delve into the detailed political economy of planned environmental transformation. This is not because the topic is unimportant but rather that in social science investigations, as in all forms of scientific inquiry, it is often indispensable to isolate the object of study in order to make it more readily understandable. The changes undergone by the territory of the island republic are only one part of an extremely ambitious project: the Singapore experiment, the Singapore model one could say, has territorial, financial, political, and even ideological ramifications that extend far beyond the borders of the 720 sq km city-state. These are definitely beyond the scope of the present study.

Our original hypothesis was that, among members of a community, even a national community, territorial instability, or better still territorial alienation can become tools of social and political control and alienation. As stated in our introduction, these cannot be readily measured. Nevertheless, we feel we have been able to show that the hypothesis has an explanatory potential worthy of further investigation and debate. In view of the pace at which the Singapore environment, the stage of an unprecedented experiment in political and social construction, continues to change, the country is appropriate testing ground.

Appendix 1: Dates and Events

2nd C. In his *Geography*, Ptolemy of Alexandria mentions the port of Sabara (or Sabana), which could have been located on Singapore island.

14th C. Singapore island is the site of an influential Malay maritime city.

1819 Stamford Raffles establishes a trading post in the name of the *East India Company*.

1824 The British formally acquire the island from the Sultan of Johor.

1826 The *Straits Settlements*, which includes Singapore, is formed.

1865 Transfer of control over the Straits Settlements from the British East India Company to the British Colonial Office.

1869 Opening of the Suez Canal.

1923 Beginning of the development of the Sembawang air and naval base.

1929 Opening of the Seletar air base.

1938 Opening of the King George VI Dry Dock.

1938 Construction of the Tengah air base.

1942 Singapore is captured by the Japanese Armed Forces (15 February).

1945 Departure of Japanese occupants (September).

1958 Singapore first Master Plan is adopted.

1959 Internal autonomy granted by the British; at the head of the People's Action Party (PAP) Lee Kuan Yew is the first Prime Minister.

1963 Integration of Singapore into the newly created Federation of Malaysia.

1965 Singapore leaves the federation and becomes an independent republic; Lee Kuan Yew remains Prime Minister.

1967 Creation of the Association of Southeast Asian Nations (ASEAN), which includes Singapore.

1970 Adoption of the first Singapore Concept Plan, called the Ring Concept Plan.

1971 Definite closure of all British military installations.

1981 Opening of Changi airport.

1990 Goh Chok Tong succeeds Lee Kuan Yew as Prime Minister. The latter remains with the government as Senior Minister.

1997 Asian Financial Crisis.

2003 Adoption of currently followed Master Plan (after the 1958, 1975, 1980, 1985, 1991 and 1998 ones).

2003 Severe Acute Respiratory Syndrome (SARS) outbreak.

2004 Lee Hsien Loong (son of Lee Kuan Yew), succeeds Goh Chok Tong as head of the PAP and as Prime Minister. Goh Chok Tong remains with the government as Senior Minister, while Lee Kuan Yew becomes Minister Mentor.

2005 Adoption of latest revised Concept Plan (after the 1971, 1991 and 2001 revisions).

2006 The Global Competitiveness Report ranks Singapore no. 5, ahead of the US, and only surpassed by four northern European countries.

Appendix 2: Singapore, 1959–2006

	1959	2006
Surface area (km²)	581.5	722.6
Population (Residents only)[a]		3,683,900
Population (Total)[a]	1,587,200	4,483,900
Major ethnic groups in 1957 and 2000 (%)		
Chinese	75.4	76.8
Malays	13.6	13.9
Indians	9.0	7.9
Others	2.0	1.4
Birth rate per thousand	32.9	10.1
Mortality rate per thousand	6.4	4.3
Infant mortality rate per thousand	36.0	2.6
Life expectancy	64[b]	80
Population growth (%)	4.0	1.8
Unemployment (%)	13.2	3.6
Literacy rate 15 years and above (%)	52.2[b]	95.4
GDP (Singapore $ millions)	2,150[c]	209,991
External trade (Singapore $ millions)	6,811[d]	810,483
Singapore $ to the US$	~ 0.33	~0.66

a. Total population comprises Singapore residents and non-residents. Resident population comprises Singapore citizens and permanent residents.

b. 1957

c. 1960

d. 1965

Sources: *United Nations Demographic Yearbooks* and http://www.singstat.gov.sg/

Bibliography

Map and Table Sources

Sources for the Base Maps

Department of Statistics. *Yearbooks*.

ESRI. Digital Chart of the World.

Leow Bee Geok, comp. (2001). *Census of Population 2000: Geographical Distribution and Travel*. Singapore: Department of Statistics.

Google Earth 2006.

Ministry of Defence, Mapping Unit (1958, 1966). Topographic 1: 63,360.

Ministry of Defence, Mapping Unit (1974, 1987). Topographic 1: 50,000.

1. Singapore: A Strategic Location

Map adapted from De Koninck, Rodolphe (2006). *Singapour: La cité-État ambitieuse*. Paris: Belin. Map 1, p. 19.

ESRI. Digital Chart of the World.

2. Singapore in the Midst of Historical Trade Centres

Map adapted from De Koninck (2006), Map 2, p. 23.

ESRI. Digital Chart of the World.

3. Contemporary Singapore

Google Earth 2006.

Leow (2001).

Ministry of Defence, Mapping Unit (1966). Topographic 1: 1 63,360.

Urban Redevelopment Authority (2003). "Master Plan 2003". http://spring.ura.gov.sg/dcd/eservices/sop/main.cfm?viewmpview

Wong Poh Poh (1966). *Singapore Island: Relief*. 1: 63,360.

4. Stretching the Land

Map adapted from De Koninck (2006), Map 7, p. 72.

Google Earth 2006.

Leow (2001).

Ministry of Defence, Mapping Unit (1958, 1966). Topographic 1: 63,360.

Ministry of Defence, Mapping Unit (1974, 1987). Topographic 1: 50,000.

Wong Tai-Chee and Yap Lin-Ho Adriel (2004). *Four Decades of Transformation: Land Use in Singapore, 1960–2000*. Singapore: Eastern University Press, p. 121.

5. Collecting and Stocking Water

De Koninck, Rodolphe (1992). *Singapour: Un Atlas de la Révolution du Territoire/Singapore: An Atlas of the Revolution of Territory*. Montpellier: RECLUS, p. 41.

Google Earth 2006.

Ministry of Defence, Mapping Unit (1958). Topographic 1: 63,360.

Ministry of Defence, Mapping Unit (1987). Topographic 1: 50,000.

Wong and Yap (2004), Figure 5.1B.

6. Diversifying Water Supply Sources

Department of Statistics.

Google Earth 2006.

Public Utilities Board. www.pub.gov.sg.

7. Holding on to Some Forest

De Koninck (1992), p. 49.

Bird, Michael et al. (2004). "Evolution of the Sungei Buloh-Kranji mangrove coast, Singapore". *Applied Geography* 24: 181–98.

Google Earth 2006.

Hill, R. D. (1977). "The Vegetation Map of Singapore". *Journal of Tropical Geography* 45: 27–33.

Ministry of Defence, Mapping Unit (1958). Topographic 1: 63,360.

Ministry of Defence, Mapping Unit (1987). Topographic 1: 50,000.

National Parks Board (2006). http://www.nparks.gov.sg/publishing.asp

Singapore Street Directory (2007).

Singapore Street Atlas 2005–2006.

Wong Poh Poh. (1989). "The Transformation of the Physical Environment", in K. S. Sandhu and Paul Wheatley (eds.), *Management of Success: The Moulding of Modern Singapore*. Singapore: Institute of Southeast Asian Studies, pp. 771–87.

Wong and Yap (2004), p. 121.

8. The Garden City

De Koninck (1992), p.105.

De Koninck (2006), p. 98.

Ministry of Defence, Mapping Unit (1958). Topographic 1: 25,000 (7 sheets).

Ministry of Defence, Mapping Unit (1988). *Road Map*. 1: 25,000 (4 sheets).

National Parks Board (2006). http://www.nparks.gov.sg/publishing.asp

Singapore Guide and Street Directory (1958).

Singapore Street Directory (1988).

Urban Redevelopment Authority (2002). "Parks and Waterbodies Plan". http://www.ura.gov.sg/pwbid/

9. The Sea in the City

Map adapted from De Koninck (2006), Map 3, p. 27.

Coleman, G. D. (1839). "Map of the Town and Environs of Singapore". London: John Murray.

Google Earth 2006

Singapore Street Atlas 2005–2006. Singapore: Periplus Editions.

10. Spreading Out the Population

Map adapted from De Koninck (2006), Maps 9, 10 and 12, pp. 80, 81 and 83.

Department of Statistics. *Yearbooks*.

Neville W. (1965). "The Areal Distribution of Population in Singapore", *Journal of Tropical Geography* 20: 16–25.

11. The Housing Question

De Koninck (1992), pp. 90–1.

Housing and Developent Board. *Annual Reports*.

12. Sembawang: Building a New Town

Singapore Street Directory (1991).

Singapore Street Atlas 2005–2006.

Singapore Street Directory (2007).

13. Private Quarters

De Koninck (1992), p. 95.

Singapore Guide and Street Directory (1958).

Singapore Street Directory (1988).

Singapore Street Atlas 2005–2006. Singapore: Periplus Editions.

14. Readjusting the Distribution of Ethnic Communities

Khoo Chian Kim (1983). *Census of Population 1980 Singapore*. Singapore: Department of Statistics Singapore, pp. 234–44.

Leow (2001), pp. 43–50.

15. Rationing Agriculture

De Koninck (1992), p. 53.

Agri-Food and Veterinary Authority of Singapore (2006). "Agrotechnology Parks in Singapore".

http://www.ava.gov.sg/AgricultureFisheriesSector/FarmingInSingapore/AgroTechParks/AgrotechnologyParksMap.htm

Ministry of Defence, Mapping Unit (1958). Topographic 1: 63,360.

Ministry of Defence, Mapping Unit (1987). Topographic 1: 50,000.

Wong (1989).

16. Expanding and Consolidating Industry

De Koninck (1992), p. 55.

Google Earth 2006.

Jurong Town Corporation. *Annual Reports*.

Ministry of Defence, Mapping Unit (1958). Topographic 1: 63,360.

Ministry of Defence, Mapping Unit (1987). Topographic 1: 50,000.

Urban Redevelopment Authority (2003), http://spring.ura.gov.sg/dcd/eservices/sop/main.cfm?viewmpview

Wong A. K. and Ooi G. L. (1989). "Spatial Reorganization", in Sandhu and Wheatley (eds.), pp. 788–812.

17. Jurong: From Mangrove to Industrial Estate

Google Earth 2006.

Ministry of Defence, Mapping Unit (1958). Topographic 1: 25,000 (7 sheets).

Singapore Street Atlas 2005–2006. 2004. Singapore: Periplus Editions.

Urban Redevelopment Authority (2003), http://spring.ura.gov.sg/dcd/eservices/sop/main.cfm?viewmpview

18. Petroleum Islands

De Koninck (1992), p. 63.

Atlas for Singapore (1988).

Google Earth 2006.

Ministry of Defence, Mapping Unit (1958). Topographic 1: 63,360.

Ministry of Defence, Mapping Unit (1987). Topographic 1: 50,000.

Singapore Street Atlas 2005–2006. Singapore: Periplus Editions.

Singapore Street Directory (2007). Singapore: Periplus Editions.

19. Foreign Lands for Expansion: The Riau Islands

Map adapted from De Koninck (2006), Map 8, p. 73.

Google Earth 2006

Riau Islands. Topographic 1: 500,000.

Riau Islands. Land Use 1: 700,000. Singapore: Periplus Editions.

Bintan. Land Use 1: 180,000. Singapore: Periplus Editions.

20. Foreign Lands for Expansion: Johor

Map adapted from De Koninck (2007), Map 13, p. 109.

Comprehensive Development Plan for South Johor Economic Region 2006–2025. Kuala Lumpur, Khazanah Nasional, 2006.

21. Foreign Lands for Expansion: The World

Map adapted from De Koninck (2006), Map 5, pp. 50–1.

http://www.iesingapore.gov.sg/wps/portal

http://www.mpa.gov.sg/

http://welcome.singtel.com/default.asp

http://www.singstat.gov.sg/stats/

22. Making Way for Cars

De Koninck (1992), p. 69.

Atlas for Singapore (1979). Singapore: Collins and Longman.

Nelles Verlag (1990). *Singapore.* 1: 125,000.

Singapore Street Directory (1991).

Singapore Street Atlas 2005–2006. Singapore: Periplus Editions.

Singapore Street Directory (2007). Singapore: Mighty Minds.

Wong and Yap (2004), Figure 2.2.

23. Transporting Workers

De Koninck (1992), p. 69.

Atlas for Singapore (1979). Singapore: Collins and Longman.

Nelles Verlag (1990). *Singapore.* 1: 125,000.

Singapore Street Atlas 2005–2006.

Land Transport Authority. 2006, in *Projects.* http://www.lta.gov.sg/

24. Doors Wide Open to the World

De Koninck (1992), p. 73.

Chia L. S. (1989). "The Port of Singapore", in Sandhu and Wheatley (eds.), pp. 314–36.

Google Earth 2006.

Ministry of Defence, Mapping Unit (1958). Topographic 1: 63,360.

Ministry of Defence, Mapping Unit (1987). Topographic 1: 50,000.

Ministry of Defence (2007). *The Air Force.* http://www.mindef.gov.sg/rsaf/

Maritime and Port Authority. http://www.mpa.gov.sg/

Port of Singapore Authority. *Annual Reports*.

Port of Singapore Authority. http://www.singaporepsa.com/

25. Changi: An Airport in the Sea

Google Earth 2006.

Ministry of Defence, Mapping Unit (1958). Topographic 1: 25,000 (7 sheets).

Singapore Street Atlas 2005–2006.

Urban Redevelopment Authority (2003), http://spring.ura.gov.sg/dcd/eservices/sop/main.cfm?viewmpview

26. SIA: A World Class Airline

Map adapted from: De Koninck (2006), Map 4, p. 49.

www.singaporeair.com/saa/app/saa

27. Places to Pray

De Koninck (1992), p. 99.

Ministry of Defence, Mapping Unit (1958). Topographic 1: 25 000 (7 sheets).

Singapore Guide and Street Directory (1958).

Singapore Street Directory (1988).

Singapore Street Atlas 2005–2006. Singapore: Periplus Editions.

28. Places for Burial

De Koninck (1992), p. 101.

Ministry of Defence, Mapping Unit (1958). Topographic 1: 25 000 (7 sheets).

Singapore Guide and Street Directory (1958).

Singapore Street Directory (1988).

Singapore Street Atlas 2005–2006. Singapore: Periplus Editions.

29. Places to Study

De Koninck (1992), p. 103.

Ministry of Defence, Mapping Unit (1958). Topographic 1: 25 000 (7 sheets).

Ministry of Education (1990). *Directory of Schools and Financial Institutions*.

Ministry of Education (2007). In *Education System, Post-secondary*. http://www.moe.gov.sg/corporate/post_secondary.htm

Morais, J. V. and Pothen P. P. (1965). *Educational Directory of Malaysia and Singapore*. Singapore.

Singapore Guide and Street Directory (1958).

Singapore Street Directory (1966).

Singapore Street Atlas 2005–2006. Singapore: Periplus Editions.

30. Places for Recreation

De Koninck (1992), p. 105.

Ministry of Defence, Mapping Unit (1958). Topographic 1: 25,000 (7 sheets).

Ministry of Defence, Mapping Unit (1988). *Road Map*. 1: 25,000 (4 sheets).

Singapore Guide and Street Directory (1958).

Singapore Street Directory (1988).

Singapore Street Atlas 2005–2006. Singapore: Periplus Editions.

31. Rallying Points

De Koninck (1992), pp. 108–9.

Maung T. T. (1957). *The Influence of The Community Centre on its Neighbourhood*. Singapore: University of Malaya (Social Studies).

People's Association. *Annual Reports*.

Singapore Street Atlas 2005–2006. Singapore: Periplus Editions.

32. The Tourist Trail: Orchard Road

Bartholomew-Clyde (1990). *Singapore City*. 1: 10 000.

De Koninck (1992), p. 115.

Singapore Guide and Street Directory (1958).

Singapore Street Directory (1988).

Singapore Street Directory (1991).

Singapore Street Atlas 2005–2006. Singapore: Periplus Editions.

Singapore Street Directory (2007). Singapore: Mighty Minds.

Singapore Tourist Promotion Board (1990). *Singapore Hotels*.

33. From Master Plan to Revised Model

Google Earth 2006.

Singapore Street Atlas 2005–2006. Singapore: Periplus Editions.

Singapore Street Directory (2007). Singapore: Mighty Minds.

Urban Redevelopment Authority (2003), http://spring.ura.gov.sg/dcd/eservices/sop/main. cfm?viewmpview

34. Land Use in 2005

Google Earth 2006.

Singapore Street Atlas 2005–2006.

Singapore Street Directory (2007). Singapore: Mighty Minds.

Urban Redevelopment Authority (2003), http://spring.ura.gov.sg/dcd/eservices/sop/main. cfm?viewmpview

Other Sources

Beamish, Jane and Jane Ferguson (1985). *A History of Singapore Architecture*. Singapore: Graham Brash.

Brunet, Roger (2001). *Le déchiffrement du monde*. Paris: Belin.

Brunet, Roger and Olivier Dollfus (1990). *Mondes nouveaux*, collection Géographie Universelle, vol. 1. Paris: Hachette / RECLUS.

Buchanan, Iain (1971). *Singapore in Southeast Asia: An Economic and Political Appraisal*. London: Bell and Sons.

Chan Heng Chee (1989). "The Structuring of the Political System", in K. S. Sandhu and Paul Wheatley (eds.), *Management of Success: The Moulding of Modern Singapore*. Singapore: Institute of Southeast Asian Studies, pp. 70–89.

Chia Lin Sien, Asafur Rahman and Dorothy Tay B. H., eds. (1991). *The Biophysical Environment of Singapore*. Singapore: Singapore University Press.

Chua Beng Huat (1997). *Communitarian Ideology and Democracy in Singapore*. London: Routledge.

Chua Beng Huat (2003). *Life is not Complete without Shopping: Consumption Culture in Singapore*. Singapore: Singapore University Press.

Clammer, John (1985). *Singapore: Ideology, Society, Culture*. Singapore: Chopmen Publishers.

Coless, B. E. (1969). "The Ancient History of Singapore", *Journal of Southeast Asian History* 10, 1: 1–11.

De Koninck, Rodolphe (1975). *Farmers of a City-State: The Chinese Smallholders of Singapore*. Montreal: Canadian Sociology and Anthropology Association.

De Koninck, Rodolphe (1990). "Singapore or the Revolution of Territory: Part One: the Hypothesis". *Cahiers de Géographie du Québec* 92: 209–16.

De Koninck, Rodolphe (1992). *Singapour: Un Atlas de la Révolution du Territoire/Singapore: An Atlas of the Revolution of Territory.* Montpellier: RECLUS.

De Koninck, Rodolphe (2005). *L'Asie du Sud-Est.* Paris: Armand Colin.

De Koninck, Rodolphe (2006). *Singapour: La cité-État ambitieuse.* Paris: Belin.

De Koninck, Rodolphe (2007). *Malaysia: La dualité territoriale.* Paris: Belin.

Dobby, E. H. G. (1940). "Singapore: Town and Country". *Geographical Review* 30: 84–109.

Edwards, Norman and Peter Keys (1988). *Singapore: A Guide to Buildings, Streets, Places.* Singapore: Times Books International.

Enright, D. J. (1969). *Memoirs of a Mendicant Professor.* London: Chatto and Windus.

Gamer, Robert E. (1972). *The Politics of Urban Development in Singapore.* Ithaca: Cornell University Press.

George, Cherian (2000). *Singapore. The Air-Conditioned Nation: Essays on the politics of comfort and control.* Singapore: Landmark Books.

Gomez, James (2002). *Internet Politics: Surveillance and Intimidation in Singapore.* Singapore: Think Centre.

Government of Singapore (1991). *Singapore: The Next Lap.* Singapore: Times Editions.

Gupta, Avijit and John Pitts (1992). *The Singapore Story: Physical Adjustments in a Changing Landscape.* Singapore: Singapore University Press.

Haas, Michael, ed. (1999). *The Singapore Puzzle.* London: Praeger.

Hancock, T. H. H. (1986). *Coleman's Singapore.* Kuala Lumpur: Malaysian Branch of the Royal Asiatic Society.

Hill, Ron D. (1977). "The Vegetation Map of Singapore", *Journal of Tropical Geography* 45: 27–33.

Hodder, Brian W. (1953). "Racial Groupings in Singapore", *Malayan Journal of Tropical Geography* 1: 25–36.

Humphrey, John W. (1985). *Geographic Analysis of Singapore's Population.* Singapore: Department of Statistics.

Kaye, Barrington (1960). *Upper Nanking Street, Singapore.* Singapore: Singapore University Press.

Kwa Chong Guan (2004). "From Temasek to Singapore: Locating a Global City-State in the Cycle of Melaka Straits History", in John N. Miksic and Cheryl-Ann Low Mei Gek (eds.), *Early Singapore: 1300–1819.* Singapore History Museum, pp. 124–46.

Lee Kuan Yew (2000). *From Third World to First: The Singapore Story, 1965–2000.* New York: HarperCollins.

Lefebvre, Henri (1974). *La production de l'espace.* Paris: Anthropos.

Lefebvre, Henri (1991). *The Production of Space.* Oxford: Blackwell.

Li, Tania (1989). *Malays in Singapore: Culture, Economy and Ideology.* Singapore: Oxford University Press.

Lim, William S. W., ed. (2002). *Postmodern Singapore.* Singapore: Select Publishing.

Lim, William S. W. (2004). *Architecture, Art, Identity in Singapore: Is there Life after Tabula Rasa?* Singapore: Asian Urban Lab.

Low, Linda, ed. (1999). *Singapore: Towards a Developed Status.* Singapore: Oxford University Press.

MacLeish, Kenneth and Winfield Parks (1966). "*Singapore: Reluctant Nation*", *National Geographic* 130, 2: 269–300.

Miksic, John N. (2000). "Heterogenetic Cities in Premodern Southeast Asia", *World Archaeology* 32, 1: 106–20.

Ministry of Trade and Industry (1986). *The Singapore Economy: New Directions.* Singapore.

Ministry of Trade and Industry (1991). *The Strategic Economic Plan: Towards a Developed Nation.* Singapore.

Ministry of Trade and Industry (2003). *New Challenges, Fresh Goals: Towards a Dynamic Global City. Report of the Economic Review Committee.* Singapore.

Neville, Warwick (1965). "The Areal Distribution of Population in Singapore", *Journal of Tropical Geography* 20: 16–25.

Neville, Warwick (1966). "Singapore: Ethnic Diversity and its Implications", *Annals of the Association of American Geographers* 61, 1: 236–53.

Neville, Warwick (1969). "The Distribution of Population in the Post-War Period", in Ooi Jin Bee and Chiang Hai Ding (eds.), *Modern Singapore*. Singapore: University of Singapore Press, pp. 52–68.

Ooi Giok Ling (2004). *Future of Space: Planning Space and the City*. Singapore: Eastern University Press.

Ooi Giok Ling and Kenson Kwok, eds. (1997). *City and the State: Singapore Built Environment Revisited*. Singapore: Oxford University Press.

Perry, Martin, Lily Kong and Brenda S. A. Yeoh (1997). *Singapore: A Developmental City State*. New York: John Wiley and Sons.

Quah, John S. T., ed. (1990). *In Search of Singapore's National Values*. Singapore: Times Academic Press.

Reith, G. M. (1985). *Handbook to Singapore, 1892 (Revised by Walter Makepeace in 1907)*. Singapore: Oxford University Press.

Rodan, Garry (1989). *The Political Economy of Singapore's Industrialization: National State and International Capital*. Kuala Lumpur: Forum.

Rodan, Garry (2004). *Transparency and Authoritarian Rule in Southeast Asia: Singapore and Malaysia*. London: RoutledgeCurzon.

Raffestin, Claude (1980). *Pour une géographie du pouvoir*. Paris: Librairies techniques.

Raffestin, Claude and Bresso, Mercedes (1979). *Travail, espace, pouvoir*. Geneva: l'Âge d'Homme.

Siddique, Sharon and Nirmala Pura Shotam (1982). *Singapore's Little India*. Singapore: Institute of Southeast Asian Studies.

Sandhu, K. S. and Paul Wheatley, eds. (1989). *Management of Success: The Moulding of Modern Singapore*. Singapore: Institute of Southeast Asian Studies.

Tamney, Joseph B. (1996). *The Struggle over Singapore's Soul*. Berlin and New York: Walter de Gruyter.

Tan Lee Wah (1975). "Changes in the Distribution of Population of Singapore: 1957–1970", *Journal of Tropical Geography* 40: 53–62.

Tay Kheng Soon (1989a). "The Architecture of Rapid Transformation, in K. S. Sandhu and Paul Wheatley (eds.), *Management of Success: The Moulding of Modern Singapore*. Singapore: Institute of Southeast Asian Studies, pp. 860–78.

_____ (1989b). *Mega-Cities in the Tropics: Towards an Architectural Agenda for the Future*. Singapore: Institute of Southeast Asian Studies.

Tay Kheng Soon & Akitek Tenggara (1997). *Line, Edge and Shade: The Search for a Design Language in Tropical Asia*. Singapoure: Page One Publishing.

Teo, Peggy, Brenda S. A. Yeoh, Ooi Giok Ling and Karen P. Y. Lai (2004). *Changing Landscapes of Singapore*. Singapore: McGraw-Hill.

Teo Siew Eng (1978). "Spatial Patterns of Residential Moves in an Asian City: The Singapore Experience", *Journal of Tropical Geography* 46: 86–94.

Trocki, Carl A. (2006). *Singapore: Wealth, Power and the Culture of Control*. London: Routledge.

Tuan Yi-Fu (1974). *Topophilia: A Study of Environmental Perception, Attitudes and Values*. Englewood Cliffs: Prentice Hall.

Turnbull, C. M. (1989). *A History of Singapore. 1819–1988*. Singapore: Oxford University Press.

Wee Yeow Chin and Richard Corlett (1986). *The City and the Forest: Plant Life in Urban Singapore*. Singapore: Singapore University Press.

Wheatley, Paul (1954). "Land Use in the Vicinity of Singapore in the eighteen-thirties", *Journal of Tropical Geography* 2: 63–66.

Wong, Aline K. and Ooi Giok Ling (1989). "Spatial Reorganization", in K. S. Sandhu and Paul Wheatley (eds.), *Management of Success: The Moulding of Modern Singapore*. Singapore: Institute of Southeast Asian Studies, pp. 788–812.

Wong Poh Poh (1969a). "The Surface Configuration of Singapore Island: A Quantitative Description", *Journal of Tropical Geography* 29: 64–74.

Wong Poh Poh (1969b). "The Changing Landscapes of Singapore Island", in Ooi Jin Bee and Chiang Hai Ding (eds.), *Modern Singapore*. Singapore: University of Singapore Press, pp. 20–51.

Wong Poh Poh (1989). "The Transformation of the Physical Environment", in K. S. Sandhu and Paul Wheatley (eds.), *Management of Success: The Moulding of Modern Singapore*. Singapore: Institute of Southeast Asian Studies, pp. 771–87.

Wong Tai-Chee and Yap Lian-Ho Adriel (2004). *Four Decades of Transformation: Land Use in Singapore, 1960–2000*. Singapore: Eastern Universities Press.

Yeoh, Brenda S. A. (1996). *Contesting Space: Power Relations and the Urban Built Environment in Colonial Singapore*. Singapore: Oxford University Press.

Yeoh, Brenda S. A. and Shirlena Huang (2004). "Foreign Talent in our Midst: New Challenges to Sense of Community and Ethnic Relations in Singapore", in Lai Ah Eng (ed.), *Beyond Rituals and Riots: Ethnic Pluralism and Social Cohesion in Singapore*. Singapore: Eastern Universities Press, pp. 316–38.

Yeung Yue-Man (1973). *National Development Policy and Urban Transformation in Singapore*. Chicago: University of Chicago.

Useful Websites

www.economist.com/countries/Singapore

www.gov.sg

www.mas.gov.sg/masmcm/bin/pt1Home.htm

www.mpa.gov.sg

www.singstat.gov.sg

www.straitstimes.asia1.com.sg

About the authors

Rodolphe De Koninck is Professor of Geography at the Université de Montréal, where he also holds the Canada Chair of Asian Research. Julie Drolet is an MA student and Marc Girard a cartographer and GIS specialist in the Geography Department in the same university.